THE GESTALT ART EXPERIENCE

THE GESTALT ART EXPERIENCE

JANIE RHYNE

BROOKS/COLE PUBLISHING COMPANY
MONTEREY, CALIFORNIA

A Division of Wadsworth Publishing Company, Inc.

ISBN: 0-8185-0102-2
L.C. Catalog Card No.: 73-84603
Printed in the United States of America
1 2 3 4 5 6 7 8 9 10—77 76 75 74 73

Production editor: Mara Robezgruntnieks-Niels
Interior and cover design: Linda Marcetti
Front cover photograph: Marvin Vickers
Back cover photograph: Carolyn Stenzler
Typesetting: Holmes Typography, Inc., San Jose, California
Color insert: Creative Repro Color Photo Lithographers,
    Monterey, California
Printing and binding: The Maple Press Company,
    York, Pennsylvania

Preface

The Gestalt Art Experience describes how to use art media to discover and explore unique personal qualities in yourself and others. It encourages you to extend your range of perception by creating forms with art materials and learning to understand the visual messages of these forms.

This book suggests structures and techniques that can be used in therapy, in growth-oriented groups, or individually. I have used art therapeutically both in therapy-oriented settings with disturbed individuals and in the art classroom with students of all ages. I have also used art with fully functioning individuals and groups and self-directed people who were seeking ways to realize more of their potential. I describe these experiences to encourage you—the individual who wants more awareness and perceptiveness—to experiment on your own with art experience; I offer ways for you to begin, whether you are a therapist, counselor, teacher, student, or client.

This book is divided into four parts. Part I outlines the theoretical basis for gestalt art experience; it also describes my use of art as I was growing up and the growth I've shared with others through art media.

Part II discusses the role of art experience in enabling people to create visual imagery that expresses repressed memories, perceptions, and living patterns; these expressions then become referents that can facilitate communication between one's inner and outer consciousness.

Part III suggests projects for individual exploration of self-perceptions, attitudes, the patterns of one's life, and the possibilities in one's future.

Part IV describes group art experiences. I give some suggestions to group leaders and describe some dynamic experiences in which art materials served to elicit expressions of the reality of our human drama.

For the last decade I have concentrated my energy on leading what I call art experience groups. I have led hundreds of sessions in the United States and some in Europe. The participants in these groups have come from a wide range of cultural and educational backgrounds: teen-agers from the ghetto, psychiatric staffs from institutions, drug users from a free clinic, housewives from suburbia, patients in psychotherapy, members of religious groups, artists, teachers, clergymen, social workers, students, nurses, and therapists. It is from these art experiences that I write.

This book and my work are based on some assumptions. I assume that the experience of creating art contributes to clarity of insight, whether the creator is a skilled artist or a sincere amateur. I assume that the experience of perceiving the visual imagery of ourselves and others contributes to breadth of understanding whether the perceiver is a professional people-helper or a layman.

I believe that too many of us spend our lives in uneasy and resentful slavery, halfheartedly trying to accept the demands of our families, our positions, our culture. Our fear keeps us immobilized; we are afraid even to question, much less defy, the value system imposed on us by our society; we fear the loneliness of autonomy. Only when we trust our individual perceptions and take action can we begin to realize some of our unique potential.

Each of us is responsible for choosing and making his individual acts against whatever deadens and for whatever enlivens. We might think that taking an active stance in any small way couldn't possibly make a difference. So we continue to allow others to make our world for us, and then we complain that we don't like our world or our life. We can resign ourselves and endure what we allow to be imposed on us or we can begin the process of creative autonomy by recognizing our individual rights and responsibilities as fellow world-makers.

In our modern culture, there is much to rebel against; we are bewildered by the complexity of our problems and possibilities. What can you or I do? We can start from where we are; we can accept ourselves as we are and our world as it is; we can use whatever resources we have to actualize the greatest possibilities available to us. Edward C. Whitmont describes what is likely to happen when

> . . . one's aspirations are so great and uncompromising that in actual reality nothing or only very little can be achieved.

For realization in the here and now requires a renunciation of the infiniteness of the many possibilities of the intuitive Great Vision for the sake of its finite and few limited aspects which, through concentration and work, can be made concrete. This problem was posed to a young patient in the following dream: "I wanted to board a bus but had no money to pay the 15¢ fare because I was not willing to break a five-dollar bill. Consequently, I was thrown off the bus." If the ego fails to give its energies to the seemingly small and limited tasks at hand because it wants to deal with only big ideas, then it cannot move on, it misses the bus, and the personality is not ready for the next phase. . . .[1]

I encourage us to break up our unusable large bills into whatever small change we need to begin reaching our goals. I affirm the value of the seemingly small journeys, of simple acts.

Most of us want to use our best selves in living, yet most of us do not use our potential for creating the kinds of lives we want. We put off doing the little things that could further our aspirations, shrugging off our hopes, saying to ourselves that they're not very important anyway. Thus, of course, we deny our individual importance.

In this book I suggest a wealth of ways we can enrich our lives. If you choose to explore some of them, know before you do that you may encounter yourself in a way that you have not done before. Know that this is not a parlor game. You may find joy, ecstasy, tremendous release. You may have fun. You may also contact pain, agony, and ugliness. This is a low-risk way of getting into high-risk areas. Please believe that I speak seriously when I ask you to accept your responsibility to honor your own feelings and those of others; to be aware of the danger of imposing on yourself and others pressures too destructive to bear. Destruction is sometimes desirable and necessary, but when and where and what to destroy is often a crucial choice; it is not one to be made casually and irresponsibly.

This is a meandering chronicle of a psychological journey with myself and others. It is not a scientific treatise proving the value of art therapy, but hundreds of people are as convinced as I am that these art experiences are enlightening and enlivening. Their discoveries and mine show the kind of treasure trove that is available to everyone who wants to enjoy, learn, and grow through participating in the gestalt art experience.

Janie Rhyne

[1] Edward C. Whitmont, *The Symbolic Quest* (New York: G. P. Putnam's Sons, 1969), pp. 281–282.

Contents

Foreword

Joen Fagan

When we think of communication—whether it is with other people or with ourselves—we usually think of words: spoken, written, or welling up inside our heads. These are the means, it seems, by which the really important messages get sent. In order to facilitate communication, both with others and with ourselves, therapy has traditionally relied on words. The patient talks, the therapist listens, the therapist talks. . . .

However, Freud made his major contributions to both personality theory and therapy by listening to messages other than the obvious, straightforward verbal messages. By focusing on dreams, images, hallucinations, slips of the tongue—all messages formerly dismissed by science as meaningless or unimportant—he opened up a new language with deep power to assist in understanding personality. Even though his treatment was labeled "the talking cure," he insisted that his patients report their dream images too, which he declared to be the "royal road to the unconscious." He also applied his new language to understanding creative persons, and he did extensive analyses of the images produced by great artists such as da Vinci and Michelangelo in their paintings and sculpture. It seems it would have been a short step for Freud to ask his patients to express themselves in graphic as well as

Dr. Joen Fagan is Professor of Psychology and Director of Clinical Training at Georgia State College; she also practices privately, working with individuals and families. Her enthusiastic interest in innovative research, especially in the area of clearer perception and communication, contributes to the creativity of her students and colleagues.

verbal form, yet he never took that step; he continued to study images in his efforts to understand personality but to use words to assist personality change.

So, following Freud, other therapists made little or no effort to use art or other nonverbal techniques to facilitate growth. Even the few therapists, such as Naumberg, who encouraged patients to express themselves in various art media still usually saw art as valuable for assisting the therapist to understand the patient's problems or progress, or for generalized catharsis, as when a child who was rigid or suppressing anger might, in play therapy, be encouraged to use finger paints to "make a mess."

On the other hand, instruction in art—sometimes a part of occupational therapy, sometimes labeled art therapy—began appearing in mental hospitals in the 1940s and 1950s. The early art therapist was often a person with training in art media whose function was to provide rudimentary instruction in techniques to patients. This was to keep the patient soothed by encouraging him to copy landscapes, religious figures, and so on; to fill time; or to allow him to express emotions in a presumably nonthreatening way. If the patient did produce something meaningful or personal, it would be sent to his therapist or ward physician, who would probably note it; with rare exceptions, that would be that.

As art therapists gained experience and sophistication, they began to experiment with using art in ways that might be genuinely growth producing. As this was happening over the last decade, many therapists became increasingly interested in artistic expression. This interest was largely a function of the human-potential movement and the various therapy approaches that were closely associated with it. Gestalt therapy especially encouraged therapists to be aware of nonverbal methods of expression and understanding. Perls, himself a painter, often used artists and dancers in his professional training workshops to provide expressive experiences for the participants. In addition, creative and performing artists became involved in the growth movement, and therapists became increasingly appreciative of applications of various artistic approaches to human achievement.

Art therapy, at last, can claim to be a genuine discipline in its own right, having characteristics of both art and therapy, but also forming its own gestalt and having its own identity. With this book, art therapy comes of age, having gone beyond the limitations of focusing on skills or artistic products, or conversely, of using art simply in the service of understanding personality. Now we witness the development and facilitation of alternative forms of communication by a person who is familiar with a variety of media and can choose appropriate ways of assisting expression and provoking growth.

Art therapy, as presented here, can be used with normal persons who wish primarily to explore new ways of expression and enjoyment as well as with the severely disturbed for whom all usual channels of communication are blocked. Age, background, or level of artistic skills present no barriers or limitations. Even a superficial reading of this book will reveal the abundant values of art therapy. A partial listing includes the facilitation of fantasy, sharpened visual perception, recognition of emotional states, development of alternative forms of expression, breaking rigid patterns, saying forbidden things, increased self-understanding, recognition and resolution of routine anxieties and dissatisfactions, explorations of time, space, and community in new ways, explorations with relationships, the quiet satisfaction of extending abilities, and the enjoyment of play.

Finally, approaches to and techniques of art therapy are only part of what is presented. Janie Rhyne also presents herself—directly, honestly, yet unobtrusively. Her description of her efforts to use and integrate her experiences and knowledge, to blend her art training with her therapeutic skills, to reintegrate gestalt psychology (which, after all, started as a theory of visual perception) with the more therapeutic approach to gestalt therapy, are eloquent examples of how to listen to oneself, to experiment, to persist, to find one's own style. It is clear that her contributions to art therapy cannot in any way be separated from her skills as a person.

I cannot imagine anyone—therapist, artist, art therapist, people-helper, person—reading this book without finding something of value.

Foreword

Joseph Downing

The Gestalt Art Experience is a major addition to the growing literature of gestalt therapy. Refreshing in its optimistic reading of life's potentialities, this rich volume is based on the author's sound, sensitive examination of her own life and professional development joined with the interacting experiences of the many, varied persons with whom she has worked. In the years I have been lucky enough to know Janie Rhyne, I have enjoyed and valued her consistent skill in producing a reasonable and ordered life for herself in even the most tumultuous settings. As in her life, so in this book, her balanced generosity fits her professional gift neatly to our needs, producing clarity and order without pedantry or obsessiveness. Her writing illuminates the obscure in personal process so that she often earns from me that response of approval, my unspoken "Of course, it must be just that way!"

My first experience with art therapy 20 years ago didn't move me to applause. Diversion it seemed, yes; but therapy, no. The focus of the artistic procedure was on the product, not the process. We three—patient, artist, and therapist—looked at the end result, the product, which was usually a tasteless amateur dabble and made hollow interpretations, which we fancied were in the tradition of Freud. I hope we

Dr. Joseph Downing is a psychiatrist in private practice in Palo Alto, California, and the President of Arica Training in America. For many years, he was director of a county mental health program. To his medical background, he later added extensive training in gestalt therapy methods, with special emphasis on healthy physical functioning. He recently joined the Arica Training program, which focuses on conscious evolution through methods derived from Eastern and Western disciplines and contemporary psychology.

may now be excused for not realizing that our formal psychotherapy often was as hollow and feckless as our art therapy. Then, the art therapist was an ancillary therapist, a lesser being who functioned as handmaiden to the exalted psychiatrist-psychotherapist. Today, Janie Rhyne is a fully mature senior gestalt therapist in her own right who focuses on the total therapy process with a competence that I personally envy. She orchestrates and directs the individual and the group toward consummating the total *process* of interaction between their inner, outer, and social selves through the materials chosen for manipulation.

Her discussions of the choice of materials, their preparation for meeting the needs of each situation, and the absolute necessity for adapting environmental factors to the individual personality contain the clearest directions for fitting the needs of the person being guided that I have ever read: "My best way of teaching and of doing therapy is to be as relaxed and aware and alert as possible, to receive cues. . . ." Excellent advice for any type of helping or educative relationship! To learn to use the eye as competently as the ear in receiving cues to the gestalt configurations being manifested is, at present, difficult. Perhaps this skill is best taught by one trained in the visual modalities, by a graphic artist. Certainly, Janie Rhyne is pre-eminent in my experience in this complex skill. To her added credit, in this volume she has successfully converted her visual expertise to the written word.

Books can be written from the guts, the heart, the mind, or the soul. Successful books must express at least one center; books of singular competence at least two. I feel this volume is the balanced expression of all four centers of personality. In that unique balance lies the central strength of both the author and her book; this balance recommends the book beyond the limits of either the adjunctive therapy world or those who are professionally interested in gestalt therapy.

In our time of speeding diversity, the necessity for recalling and gaining our center grows on us. Janie Rhyne has found her center from which she can sense the central potential with us all. She dares "to envision what can be." She presents a method to attain it. I recommend to you the author, her vision, and her method.

THE
GESTALT
ART
EXPERIENCE

Part One

ART EXPERIENCE IN THERAPEUTIC GROWTH PROCESSES

Chapter One

WHAT IS THE GESTALT ART EXPERIENCE?

A GESTALT FRAMEWORK

The word *gestalt* is German and has no exact equivalent in English. *Form, figure, pattern, structure,* and *configuration* are possible translations, but none is quite right, so we have adopted *gestalt* into English and bandy it about quite a bit in various contexts.

I bandy the word about in the context of the art experience. There is gestalt psychology and gestalt therapy, and there is the gestaltist's way of perceiving himself and others—a way of being, acting, and integrating experience. The premises of gestalt philosophy most relevant to the art experience seem so natural and so consistent with my attitudes that I find it hard to distinguish between what are gestalt tenets and what are my own personal apprehensions of how we human beings become and are.

Healthy children are naturally gestaltists—they live in the present; give full attention to what they are doing; do what they want to do; trust their own experiential data; and, until they are trained out of it, they know what they know with direct simplicity and accuracy.

Most of us are not allowed to grow up naturally, to learn through experience, to add to our knowledge without losing our naive wisdom: our parents, teachers, and culture coerce us into conforming to the accepted standards of how we should feel, think, and do. With varying degrees of stubbornness we resist and then gradually put away our own individual sensibilities and accept our educators' ideas about

3

what a person ought to be. During this process we are forced to deny much of what we know to be true about our own nature. We want approval and acceptance. Most of us, by the time we are considered adult and mature, have forgotten how to be ourselves. We remember just enough of what being ourselves feels like to be afraid of it. Our fear keeps us in a state of tension or deadness so we spend most of our lifetime performing instead of living and use most of our energy denying our fear of knowing ourselves and each other deeply and wholly.

Gestaltists offer ways to get through this wall of fear—we seek ways to recognize what we have hidden away—and to integrate our disowned parts into our total personality. We work to break through the barriers separating our authentic selves from the artificial roles we play. This isn't easy to do since we assumed these roles (probably during childhood) for defense, praise, attention, avoidance, or power.

Perhaps as children we knew we were only pretending to act in a certain way to get whatever it was we needed or wanted, but when the pretense was successful, we continued to play that game until we fooled even ourselves into believing that our phoniness was genuine.

Now we are adults, supposedly mature and functioning adequately, but with sneaking suspicions that we are not what we seem to be; that if we aren't careful, other people will see through our game; or worse yet, that we ourselves will realize how trite and shoddy is the show we put on.

When some situation in living forces our secret self-doubts out into the open, we have alternatives: we can commit suicide; we can find another self-delusion; we can continue the same boring games, knowing that we are dead; or we can begin the courageous search for finding in ourselves what is genuine. We can learn to give up falseness and grow into realness.

Some people say that change from phony-self to authentic-self can happen quickly and completely in some situations. Maybe, but I am dubious.

For me and for people with whom I share this experience of unlearning and regrowth, I find this is a process rather than a happening. We are active in the process, individually responsible for finding our various ways of re-creation of ourselves. No one way is *the* way.

For myself I choose a variety of ways, but the most effective for me is to use art materials to make images that allow me to rediscover not only some of the simple, naive wisdom of the child that I was but provide me with a visual imagery that evokes associations, resonances, and insights that are available to me if I just take the time to become aware of them. If I make a drawing of my fantasies, I can see them, I can read my messages, I can learn; I can integrate my past childhood with my present and with visions of my future. I think of my expressive drawings as sources of learning serving me somewhat as my dreams do. These are different from the dreams I experience during sleep but alike in that both kinds of imagery can provide a path not only into the suppressed feelings of me as a child but also into present recognition of what I need and want now. They show how I, as a mature person, can bring all of these realizations together into the pattern of my own gestalt, whose every part is related to the total configuration that is me—past, present, future—and that I and my environment are ever-changing and ever-interacting.

EXPERIENCE ART GESTALT

Recently the term *gestalt* has been applied to so many kinds of activities that it seems to have become a sort of mumbo-jumbo magic password to get some people onto a popular bandwagon. I am glad that a gestaltist approach is widely accepted now; I am sorry when it is sold by a traveling medicine man who spiels his formula as a panacea—cheap to buy, easy to take, and guaranteed to cure whatever ails you. I regret this presentation not only because it is false but also because the patented, sold-in-a-bottle, come-on pitch turns many truly thoughtful people away from seeing and knowing for themselves the genuine substance of gestalt psychology and gestalt therapy.

Now I must define simply what I mean by the gestalt art experience. This combination of words has become meaningful to me; I have chosen the three of them to describe a process that makes sense beyond the boundaries of any verbal definition. But I must use the words to make sense, too; each word is a symbol for many cultural and personal ideas. Too often, when we are communicating verbally, we take for granted that we are each using the same word-symbols to represent exactly the same ideas. Too often we thus mis-communicate and get hopelessly caught in semantic morasses that hide our meanings behind different usages.

Let me define what I mean by the gestalt art experience by discussing each word separately. The last word, *experience,* comes first, just as experience comes first in any self-involving process.

Experience, says Webster's, is "the act of living through an event or events; personal involvement in or observation of events as they occur." Each time you and I draw, paint, or model we are actively living through an event: our own experiential event. Every line you draw is uniquely yours; the ones I draw are individually mine; each of us is involved in a personal happening. As the lines and shapes emerge from our activity, we can observe how we are forming a visible graphic record of some thing or sensation that we perceive. Having recorded that perception we each have a tangible reality to use as we prefer. You can denigrate your drawing with, "Oh well, it's not very good.

I never could draw, anyway." You can deny your expression with, "That drawing doesn't mean anything to me." You can disown the form you've made with, "It just came out that way. I didn't have anything to do with it. That's not the way I see and feel."

But your drawing *does* have a lot to do with you—with the way you see and feel and think and with the way you perceive. When you do an art activity, you are experiencing yourself; what you produce comes not from a depersonalized "it" but from a very personalized you. Your personal art expressions deserve your attention.

Perhaps you've never known an art activity as a real experience—not since you were a child, anyway, and maybe you don't remember scribbling lines and smearing shapes on any handy surface. That was a real experience, but maybe you were punished or persuaded out of that kind of expression. And so you've forgotten that you once knew how to draw freely and experience your delight, anger, and all kinds of living rhythms without self-consciousness. If so, think of the kinds of unself-conscious things you still do—dancing, singing, arranging furniture, choosing your clothes, and all the other ways you express your personal self. And think of your dreams, both sleep-time and daytime weavings of your fantasies. All of these are events that involve you personally and that you can observe as they occur.

So that's how I use the word *experience:* dreaming, feeling, thinking, acting, expressing, and being aware at the same time that you are the person who is doing all of this.

How am I using the word *art*? I turn to Webster's again and find "human ability to make things; creativity of man as distinguished from the world of nature."

Making things is natural to man; perhaps we became human as we made things. Like our primitive ancestors, we make ourselves shelter, food, clothes, and transportation. Like the cave people, we use a lot of time and energy providing ourselves with more or less of those basics according to our experiences and perceptions of what our basic needs are. How need-satisfactions—physical, cultural, and psychological—evolve from direct survival necessities to luxurious desirables is too complex to discuss here. Very simply, all cultures and the individuals in them have needs beyond survival needs; these additional needs are often called "wants." I make no clear distinction between need and want because when I want something strongly enough, I presume that I need it.

I am presuming, then, that humans both need and want to make things—to do art. That desire is an inherent part of our humanity. We use that desire in many different ways, with various degrees of facility and for various ends, but we all do it in one way or another. I believe that we want to and need to if we are seeking our fullest humanity. There are those who disagree; they say, "You are just believing that because you want to. You need some sort of idealism, so

you put your faith in man's basic creative urge. You can't prove it!"
I hear their arguments—sometimes smugly, thinking I know better,
sometimes with sadness, fearing that they are right. However, until
some of the "if you can't measure it, you can't believe it" adherents
can come up with a better answer, I'll trust my own perceptions and
observations. From prehistoric times until today, we have made things
that didn't exist before; we have put things and ideas together, presenting a synthesis; we have created symbols and communicated
meanings.

I don't know why we do this; I do know that we do. So I start
from that assumption and find excitement in exploring how we can perceive and create and communicate better through the media of the
forms that we make. So, by *art,* I mean the forms that emerge from our
individual creative experiencing.

I originally used the word *gestalt* to relate my orientation in
art experience to the assumptions of gestalt psychologists.

I discovered gestalt psychology after years of doing art—
years that involved much experimenting and exploring and trusting in
my own perceptions. My discovery of the theories of gestalt psychology
was very exciting because it created a theoretical bridge between
what I knew of my processes in art-making and what I perceived in
other people's art and life processes.

I had known that various schools of psychotherapy had used
art as an auxiliary method for diagnosis, for expression of so-called
unconscious material, for emotional release, and as occupational
therapy. Not until I encountered gestalt psychology did I find support
for my belief that the art experience could be a primary, direct,
conscious mode of acting out that often integrated fantasy and reality
into actuality immediately and constructively.

Basically, "gestalt psychology originated as a theory of perception that included the inter-relationships between the form of the
object and the processes of the perceiver. . . . Gestalt thinking empha-
sized 'leaps' of insight, closure, figure-ground characteristics, fluidity
of perceptual processes, and the perceiver as an active participant in
his perceptions rather than a passive recipient of the qualities of form."[1]

Not until I met Fritz Perls in 1965 did I learn that he had
applied some concepts of gestalt psychology in formulating a practice
of gestalt therapy in a way that paralleled my own applications of
gestalt psychology theories in the kind of art experience work I was
doing. In training and working with Perls and other gestaltists, I learned
more about how they did what they did: they were finding ways to
facilitate therapeutic growth by showing people how to get out into

---

[1] Joen Fagan and Irma Lee Shepherd, eds., *Gestalt Therapy Now* (Palo Alto,
Calif.: Science and Behavior Books, 1970), p. 3.

the open feelings that had been walled off inside themselves, or to make explicit what had been implicit.

I realized that I was doing that, too—using art media as a bridge between inner and outer realities, encouraging people to create their own visual art forms and to use these as messages they send to themselves. Made visible, the messages can be perceived by their maker; since sender and receiver are the same person, the chances of perceiving a whole pattern—a gestalt—are worth betting on.

The kinship between gestalt theories of perception and their applications in art experience is obvious to me. The psychologist speaks of perceiving whole configurations as being more than the sum of the parts that make up that whole. The artist knows that it is the relationships of the parts within the whole of any art form that create the meaningful effect; looking at each part separately gives an entirely different impression from perceiving the patterned whole. The gestalt psychologist says that we tend to see similar shapes, lines, and colors as belonging together, so we perceive them as creating a visual group and thus form a figure that stands out in awareness from a less figural background. We tend to perceive continuity in lines and shapes even when there are gaps in the actual visual material that we see; we naturally seek to make wholes out of parts. We feel frustrated when we see things that seem incomplete. When we look at a form that is almost a circle, we tend to perceive a complete circle—that is, our perceptions tend to complete a shape, thus creating closure of that form.

These principles of gestalt perception become easily comprehensible when we experience their application in the process of creating our own art forms. Experientially we can perceive immediately that a number of colored shapes seen as unrelated parts have little effect; if we put them together into an integrated composition, we see a whole that is obviously greater than the sum of the parts. Similarly, when we represent imagery with graphic media, we naturally create figures and backgrounds. In using art media we discover, too, our own tendency toward completing wholes and effecting closure of unfinished parts of wholes. We become aware of the patterns within the configuration, too. We recognize that we are visually selective, since we are more likely to perceive clearly some forms than others. In the art experience, we gain insight into how we perceive generally and how our perceptions are influenced by our individual personalities.

The way we perceive visually is directly related to how we think and feel; the correlation becomes apparent when we represent our perceptions with art materials. The central figures we depict emerge from a diffuse background and give us clues as to what is central in our lives. The way we use lines, shapes, and colors in relationship to each other and to the space we put them in indicates something about how we pattern our lives. The structure or the lack of it in our forms is related to our behavior in living situations.

Realizing how we use our visual perception in creating art forms can give us new insights into how we can use our perceptiveness to create more integrated lives.

So, *gestalt,* as I use it here, means the ability to perceive whole configurations—to perceive your personality as a totality of many parts that together make up the reality of you.

Gestalt art experience, then, is the complex personal you making art forms, being involved in the forms you are creating as events, observing what you do, and hopefully perceiving through your graphic productions not only yourself as you are now, but also alternate ways that are available to you for creating yourself as you would like to be.

That's how I describe the work I do now. When I began doing this sort of thing as a child, I didn't call it work, and I gave no name to my activities. I just did what came naturally.

MY PRIVATE IMAGERY

I began consciously using the art language by graphically expressing feelings that I knew were not acceptable to people around me and that were definitely not compatible with the image I presented to the world. I didn't want anyone to see what I was doing except me.

As a skinny, pale, freckled, myopic, and dreamy little girl, I lived on at least two levels, both of which were very real. The oldest child in a large, intense family, I had responsibilities requiring more maturity than I was capable of, but I assumed the role of "little mother" nonetheless and was praised for being a good, loving, understanding big sister—most of the time, anyway. That was my outside image, the way I think most people saw me, and the way I could act openly with pride and some self-righteousness.

I took pride in my inside life, too, but about that suppressed part of me, I was very secretive. In my inner world I wasn't anyone's daughter or sister or mother, and I wasn't good or loving or understanding at all.

The outside, good-little-girl me took art lessons from Miss Helen and painted some pretty pictures to hang on the wall. Miss Helen taught me how to copy other people's paintings, how to do pleasant still-lifes and landscapes. I liked working with the materials, and though I had sneaking suspicions that copying was like cheating, still I felt virtuous and pleased that my paintings were framed and admired. I accepted with gratitude my family's pronouncement that I was talented and would probably be an artist when I grew up. Somehow "being an artist" made it seem all right to me that I had a whole secret life that didn't fit with my behavior in the actual world.

Miss Helen would have disapproved if she had ever seen what I was doing on the sly with the bit of art instruction she gave me. The private inner me drew pictures too, but these were not copies of anything I had ever seen hung on anybody's wall, and they certainly were not pretty or pleasant. No one has ever seen those drawings except me; I tore them up as soon as I made them, but I remember some of them still. Often they were fiendish drawings: dark, intertwining, murderous vine- and tree-shaped monsters; slinky gray cats waving malignant long tails while blood dribbled out of their mouths; a likeness of the little girl across the street, whom I hated, completely naked and tied tightly to a huge block of ice. I shivered when I drew that, relishing how miserably she would freeze to death.

In my inner life I was not only bad—cruel, resentful, vindictive—but I was crazy, too; I was as crazy as the loon, the bird whose desperately hysterical laughter I heard at night among the pine trees. I never saw the loon, but I could draw her as she sounded to me. I drew dark, wild trees with sharp branches tangled to make a cage for a bird who was a vague white shape trying to escape, screaming her maddened plea for freedom.

I drew exotically beautiful things, too: flowers I had never seen except in my mind's eye; dramatic desert mountains in dry, hot earth colors. I drew myself as a man riding a white horse across burning, undulating sands. I destroyed these pictures, too, but I cherished the excitement of doing them and their flamboyant content.

I was not always engaged in morbid and exotic fantasies. At times I had plain fun. Call it healthy or not, I reached an age when I became aware that sex was a reality and something I was very interested in. I vividly recall one hot summer afternoon when I was about 12 years old. My grandfather was paying me ten cents an hour to take care of his office while he did business errands. I sat at his rolltop desk and found yellow typing paper and colored pencils in its drawers and cubicles. I found that I could use the red pencils on the yellow pages to make flesh tones. I started drawing lush, fleshy people—naked men and women. I got more daring. I put sex into my drawing. My information was scanty, but my imagination ran riot. I was drawing all that I could fantasize of sexual orgies.

I enjoyed every minute of my tingling sensuality. I was representing what good little girls were not supposed even to think about. I reveled in my wickedness until the clock told me that it was time for my grandfather to return. Very tidily I tore my lurid sheets into small pieces and burned them in the fireplace along with the trash from the wastepaper baskets. When Grandfather came in I was sitting primly in his big chair. He offered to buy me a chocolate soda, so we walked a block to the drugstore, and I sat demurely beside him on the tall swivel stools and sucked the syrupy liquid through a wilted straw. Grandfather loved chocolate sodas; I detested them, but I never told him so. I was a good little girl and much too polite to say no to my elders. Besides, I had already done my sinning for the day. (See Figure 1.)

Figure 1. "I Had Already Done My Sinning."

In spite of, or maybe because of, my secret sinning through art, I grew up reasonably sane and went away to college to learn how to be a real artist. There I met with learnings I had not expected. In the art department I was a dud. My obstinate insistence that I wanted to paint what I felt did not impress the teachers, and I had to struggle mightily to get decent grades. In the science department I fared quite well; physics, biology, sociology, and especially psychology fascinated me. I found that I was taking more courses in psychology than in art, and I was reading books that said more about people than about art. When I studied art history, I was somewhat sheepishly more interested in the artist as a person than I was in his paintings as museum pieces. By the time I had finished college, without consciously planning to, I had already turned toward my genuine interest in the psychology of art. But I continued to paint and found deeper satisfactions as I developed my own style. I graduated as an art major.

I was surprised to find that I had also earned a teacher's certificate in general science and psychology as well as in art. What to do with it? How to implement my idea that art and people could be closer companions?

Even after I married, I continued as a graduate student, bumbling toward my half-formed goal of taking art out of the realm of the esoteric and into the reality of daily lives. I taught design in the university and encouraged art expression in a group of pre-school children. A year later, my husband and I received scholarships to study in Germany at the University of Heidelberg. I wanted to write my thesis on a comparison of the state-controlled art of Germany and the free art of France. That was in 1937, and the Nazis weren't favorably inclined toward a brash young lady nosing around when they were using art as propaganda. We left Germany rather precipitously at the suggestion of a minor but impressively uniformed official. A confusing month in Paris confirmed my realization that I was playing around in a serious game that I did not begin to understand. After seven chaotic months in Europe, I was glad to see the Statue of Liberty again. I made a firm decision to settle down into the role of suburban housewife.

Making the conscious decision was one thing; living the role of model wife-and-mother was another. Said I to me, "It is time for you to become mature and sensible! You should give up your fanta-sizing and your art and concentrate on being practical!" My advice to me sounded good, but it didn't work very well. During 17 years of marriage I struggled to hide my sensitive little-girl self behind my mask of stolid stability. But my sensing self, whom I thought I had locked away, would not keep quiet; she kept clamoring to be let out. I could hear her, I knew she was a part of me, but I did not know how to answer my own inner voice. So my adult self took me to a psy-chotherapist.

When I walked into the psychiatrist's office, I said tremu-lously and proudly, "Listen, I need help! I think I'm quite sane, but I have all sorts of emotions that seem crazy to others. I'm not sure I believe in psychoanalysis, but I'm confused enough to try anything." I'll always be grateful for his calm and amused voice answering, "Psychoanalysis is not a religion; you don't have to take it on faith. If it works for you, that's enough. Sit down."

With my psychiatrist's perceptive guidance, my child-self and my parent-self began the process of listening to each other. Gradually I began to see the different aspects of me as parts of my wholeness; I began to integrate my personal identity to include both the child and the woman that I am.

For me, psychotherapy worked in many valuable ways. Throughout the thrice-weekly sessions, my theme was my need to express myself and live in a way that was natural for me. In trying to adjust to a cultural model, I had denied my individuality. In denying my dark fantasies, I had also denied myself access to the excitement and joy of living fully, which was also a vital part of me. The therapist consistently encouraged and supported my use of art.

The woman that I am now is not so different from the child that I was then. I still need some secret life, though I don't call it sinning anymore. One day I am weary and bored; I am thinking bitter thoughts. The beauty of sunshine, trees, and birds annoys me. I do not want beauty when I feel so ugly. I feel dark, and I want to see darkly. The ferns are growing fresh, bright green, but I want to see darkly; I want to see only the dark red poison oak coming up again after I've killed it back so brutally. There are people here whom I love and who love me; I want them to go away.

Figure 2. "Some Days I Am Ugly."

Some days I am ugly, dark, poisonous, and alienated. (See Figure 2.) And I cannot at that time honestly feel any different than I do feel. I could pretend; I could smile at people and say how beautiful the weather is, how nicely the birds sing, and praise the garden. I probably wouldn't fool my friends, though, and I would certainly not fool me. When I act like a lady while feeling like a bitch, I don't believe me at all.

So instead of acting phony, I go off by myself and try some homemade therapy. I take a lump of clay—a big one—and I throw it down hard. I make all the shapes look like I feel—ugly, hard, angry. I bang the clay around and let myself go into my wrangling. Now I make a figure of my head and I dig out a hole in the top. I feel better. I dig more. "Aha!" I say to me. "My head is filled with a lot of useless worrying again. Time to stop computing my future debts. Time to clear my head out." No miracle happens; I haven't solved any momentous problems. I have simply given myself a bit of awareness and found that my ugliness was in my own head, not outside among my friends in the sunshine. "No need to throw my anger at them when they are not my target! Better dig at my clay figure than into my friends when they don't have the answers I need. Today is a time for me to withdraw and own up to what is mine alone."

After my time of withdrawing into my private art experience, I come back into contact with my friends. (See Figure 3.) Having expressed my negative feelings with the clay, I relax now and accept what is positive in our world of person-to-person relationships.

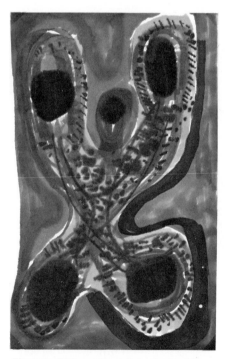

Figure 3. "I Come Back into Contact."

My use of art in my private life is not always to relieve feelings of anger or ugliness. Sometimes I want to use art simply to express emotions that cannot be put into words—for example, a dizzying ecstasy that can't be explained coherently to anyone else. One

night after an overstimulating evening, I was alone and seemed about
to explode with exhilaration. So I spent several hours painting a
brilliantly colorful vortex of excitement. That painting hangs on my
wall now; sometimes when I feel dull I go to it for rejuvenation.

I paint puzzling, painful, and exotic dreams, too—those I am
too embarrassed, still, to share with others and those that I want to
clarify for myself. Most of the time I can discriminate between what I
want to express privately with art and what I want to speak of ex-
plicitly to others.

When I was a child I trusted my perceptions of what I needed
for me because I was naive. Now I trust because I am seasoned by
living. The seasoning has not occurred without stretching and pain.
During my psychotherapy I recognized that I must accept myself as I am
and go on from there; the loon tangled in tree branches, the one I had
drawn as a child, was appearing again in my paintings. I could no longer
deny my empathy with her; I felt trapped and knew that I had to find
my way out of those dark, wild trees of self-denial. With guilty sadness
I got a divorce, and with many trepidations I packed two suitcases, took
two dogs and my children—one of them me—and went back to graduate
school again. Once again my studies included not only art but people-
oriented cultural anthropology. I received my M.A. 20 years after my
B.A. The children and I went off to live in an artists' community in
Mexico. In a 10-year close relationship with a second husband who was
a dedicated artist, I learned much more firsthand about artists as people.

Because of my exploring, I discovered through actual experience how I can facilitate people's use of art media for their own expression, communication, contact, and problem solving. Though my
exploration is experimental and pragmatic, it is based on my belief that
all of us, unless we are severely psychically or physically crippled,
are intrinsically creative; that we are as gods and do create ourselves
and our communities out of what is available to us. Much more is available than our prosaic minds will dare to admit. We have many alternative
ways of behaving and being. We are involved in cultural evolution,
maybe revolution, and each of us is responsible for his part in our total
evolution as humans. My part is small and so is yours, but all our little
parts, together, make the configuration, and the whole is greater than
the summation. That philosophy is a basis for the way I live and work;
philosophy is dead unless it is lived.

Chapter Two

THERAPEUTIC EXPERIENCES WITH ART

TEACHING AND LEARNING
WITH CHILDREN

Just as I refuse to describe people's experiences as case histories, I am reluctant to call myself an art therapist; I prefer to say that I am a person whose living includes being with others as friend, as teacher, as student, and sometimes as therapist and that all of these relationships are continually shifting; that is, the "who is doing what to whom" relationship remains ambiguous. I began to accept this idea professionally when I first taught art and science in a small understaffed private school.

My class of nine children had been grouped together mostly because none of them seemed to fit anywhere else. In my attempts to teach them, I began to learn how to use art therapeutically with others.

The nine children all had problems serious enough to label them as misfits in public schools but not disturbing enough to get them into institutions. Their ages ranged from 10 to 15 years, their IQs from 70 to 160; some were in private therapy, some were not. There was no school psychologist.

I was younger then—inexperienced, idealistic, and excited by my first job, which had been obtained with that teacher's certificate that said I was competent to teach general science and art and also that I was trained in psychology. I wasn't adequately equipped, but I acted as a therapist because the situation called for a therapeutic approach. I used art as a vehicle because I was at home with that medium and because I found it worked.

It worked for some of my charges much differently than for others: all the children liked to use the art materials; most of them made discoveries for themselves; a few just puttered around and were content to paint with no great interest. Louise, whose card said "IQ 160," wasn't interested in anything much except sex and getting other people into trouble; in both areas she was precociously competent. She often cornered Tom, who was several years younger, several heads shorter, and much more innocent than she; I would rescue him from her teasing and cajoling, though I didn't know whether he appreciated or resented my interference. In midyear Louise's mother took her off to Miami Beach, and she never returned. Before leaving, she enjoyed one art experience; she persuaded Tom to pour one cupful of bright red paint into a gallon jar of pure white and then laughed triumphantly while I fumed and resisted my impulse to drown her in the pale pink liquid. I was not sorry to see Louise go; high IQ or not, she seemed to need something different from what the little group and I could provide.

With three of the children, though, the art experience became the focus of our times together. Each of them had different attitudes and needs, but they shared a fascinated interest in using art materials, so I put a lot of time and energy into devising ways for them to use the media and in observing how they benefited from different approaches. Bob, Mike, and Matilda could not tell me verbally what they needed, and I had no one to advise me. The kids and I just did the best we could, and we all learned a lot in the process.

Bob

A 12-year-old boy taught me, nonverbally, that if I did not respect his right to be silent, he would have no contact with me at all. Bob's parents told me something of his history. He had been a precocious infant, learning to talk very early. He had been sent to a private nursery school at age 2 and learned to read by the time he was 4. He learned everything faster than his peers. He was praised and tested and pushed and exhibited by his proud parents. Then, at the age of 9, Bob stopped talking; first with his father, then with his mother, and finally Bob would speak with no one. When examinations and further testing showed no physical disability, Bob was sent to a psychiatrist. He was in therapy all the time he was in my class, but I knew nothing of that part of his life and neither his parents nor his therapist knew anything about the art work Bob did. His mother and father were not interested in his drawings and paid no attention to them. I did, however, and I wanted Bob's therapist to see them, too, but his parents were defensive about the idea of his being a "patient"; they didn't want to interfere with his doctor's work, and they didn't want me doing it either, so they didn't tell me the name of his psychiatrist or anything much else after our first talk. I received their message: I was only a young art teacher, I should remain in my place, teach Bob art, keep him busy, and not bother them with my naive foolishness about his drawings being important.

So I turned my attention directly to Bob as he turned his concentration on his drawings. He was a handsome, healthy boy with clear blue eyes and a quiet, gentle smile. He sat alone at a small table, placed smooth white paper squarely in front of him, used sharp-pointed pencils and fine pen points dipped in black ink, and he drew engines! Nothing else—always engines with details meticulously and finely delineated. When the other children were noisy or made overtures toward him, he would keep them at a distance with his steady eyes and composed smile. To me, his sober eyes were always saying, "Don't come too close. I'm watching you. Don't come too close." So I kept my distance out of respect for the sturdy, defensive wall of silence Bob had built around him. I found, though, that he liked it when I looked at his drawings as long as I didn't make a big thing out of them. Finally I mustered enough courage to comment on the intricacies of the machinery in his engines and even to ask questions. I was genuinely fascinated, so I could ask with real interest, "I see that your engine runs with gears and that the power is transferred from here to there with meshing from the little gears to the big ones and then through this shaft to the wheels; but I don't know what that part is." "That's a cam," Bob answered. He spoke without effort. After some months, he explained other parts in his drawings.

I have forgotten the mechanics he taught me, but I'll never forget my quiet joy when the tone of his voice expressed some aliveness even though his words spoke only of the structures and functions of machines. We never talked about Bob as a person. When my comments and questions got anywhere near the personal he would give me his hard stare, and I would become as quiet as he. At the end of the year Bob was transferred to another private school; several years later his close-mouthed parents told me, "He is doing quite well."

"Doing *what* quite well?" I wondered but didn't ask. I learned more questions than answers in my relationship with Bob and his parents. Bob's parents seemed to have mouths like snapping turtles; I could fantasize them biting down hard and refusing to let go. They were hard-shelled, too, and I knew no way to reach them. Did Bob feel that way about them, too? During the years when he refused to use words, what was he thinking? What complexity of thinking-feeling was he expressing in his intense involvement with engines? Was it coincidental that his father was an ambitious, prominent engineer? Did Bob show his engine world to his therapist, or has he kept gears and wheels and shafts for himself alone? At least he let me see them. I think he trusted me to receive his symbolic message because, instead of pushing him into performing according to any standardized achievement goals, I respected him enough to let him use the art media in his own way. Nor did I try to push him into speaking until he was ready to speak.

Mike

Bob's stillness and quietness had drawn my attention to him. Another boy clamored for my attention with his continuous movement and noise.

Mike was 13 years old when I met him. During a long illness four years before, he had been kept at home under the constant surveillance of his apparently doting parents. His mother, tight-lipped and hard-eyed, told me that he had Saint Vitus' Dance and was driving her crazy; she loved him very much, but she didn't know what to do with him. I didn't either during those first weeks. Mike was tall, gangly, and eternally in motion, disrupting any and all activities indiscriminately. He liked to paint, so I let him do that no matter what the other children were doing. His concentration was intense as long as he was slopping bright colors on a sheet of paper, never defining any shapes, always brushing on brilliant colors in motion. "This is fine," I thought. "Mike is absorbed in something of his own and is leaving the other children free to do their thing." But Mike moved so fast that he soon tired of painting just his own sheet of paper. He started painting everything around him— the tables, chairs, other children's work, and their faces. Every time he did this, pandemonium broke loose in shrieks, tears, and fights. I tried reasoning with Mike. He'd respond by solemnly promising to stay in his own space, but as soon as he started painting, he was off again.

In desperation, I decided to give him all the space he wanted. I bought a huge roll of wrapping paper and tacked it up on a long side of the room. I gave Mike large house-paint brushes and cheap poster paints by the quart, and then I left him alone. All I did was observe when he had finished covering the four- by thirty-foot expanse of paper and ask his help in unrolling more and pinning it to the wall. Mike dripped and splashed paint; he and the floor were a mess, but mostly he stayed in his own area. Gradually he began to discriminate between splashing paint and using paint to create forms. During the early months of that first year, Mike learned to paint murals. Toward the end of the year he joined the group more often and even took responsible leadership at times. It was he who suggested that the whole class do a mural together and proposed the theme "The History of the World," which I thought so expressive of Mike's need for a large scope. The mural was done all around the wall with each of the children participating.

The marvel was the change in Mike's attitude. Since it was *his* idea he wanted the painting done "right," so he took the lead in telling the others about staying with an overall plan, telling them with some scorn that certain areas were reserved for certain themes. "You can't paint a dinosaur right next to an airplane!" He'd developed quite a bit of firsthand knowledge about mixing colors, too, and was helpful in advising others how not to get a muddy brown when you wanted a bright purple.

The gradual change in Mike's way of working with people and materials grew out of his being allowed to act out his unrealized need for free expression. He could not use words to describe his frustrations; his verbal responses were docile and penitent: "Yes, I'll be good. Yes, I know I shouldn't mess up other people's paintings." His speaking voice was small and meek; his body and his art language shouted desperately, "I need time and space and action! Give me freedom to work in my own way!" When I saw and accepted Mike's real message, I was able to provide what he needed; he then paced his activities to answer his body's demands.

I don't know if Mike can maintain his concentration in adult life, but at least he learned to direct his energies forcefully and still keep them within acceptable and constructive limits.

Matilda

The third child who benefited from the art experience did nothing to attract my attention at first; in fact, she almost never did anything except when she was forced to. Her appearance, manner, and responses were all incredibly dull. She seemed to fade into the paint-splattered gray walls. After a while I became aware that my policy of letting the children find their own way was working in reverse with Matilda; the more I encouraged individual initiative, the more she just sat. Finally, reluctantly and impatiently, I decided to initiate projects for her. Her file card reported: "Age 14; IQ 70; difficulty in reading." I had never had close contact with a child as passive as Matilda; I didn't know how to kindle in her some sort of interest in something. I thought perhaps I could assist her in learning to read. We had an encyclopedia for children, simply written, so each time something occurred that Matilda showed any interest in, I would suggest that she read about it in the encyclopedia. With well-behaved and uninterested docility, she would look up the words, look at the pictures, study the print, and with a blank face return to just sitting. "Oh, well," I thought, "Maybe there's no way I can enliven Matilda. Maybe she's all right the way she is."

But one day we were having a lesson about breathing. I was telling the kids about the cilia in their breathing apparatus that filtered dust out of the air they breathed. Most of the children got the general idea, but they were most interested in the word *cilia*, which they promptly made *sillier* and started all sorts of hilarious punning. Matilda didn't get the point and remained quite sober. She asked, "Do I really have little hairs inside of me that sweep out the dust?" So, of course, the other kids with their casual cruelty made Matilda the butt of their jokes, chanting "Sillier! Sillier! Sillier!" For the first time, I really empathized with Matilda; she was intrigued with the idea of those little hairs inside of her; it was the first clue I had received that she could express real curiosity. So I ignored the other children, wrote down the correct spelling, and told Matilda to find the word in the encyclopedia, to read what she found there, and then tell the others what she had found. With a smile she obeyed, and then was crestfallen because the words in the encyclopedia didn't make sense to her, nor did the diagrammatic drawing of the nasal passages and trachea. She was disappointed and near tears; she wanted to understand, but the words and diagrams were too abstract for her. Suddenly I had an inspiration. "Listen," I said, "if you put your finger just inside your nose and touch very gently, you can feel some of your cilia." She did and was wide-eyed. "Now, maybe you can draw a picture of what your cilia feel like inside your nose." She did that, too, and far more happened than I could have foreseen. Her first lines were literal hairs, then she drew different kinds of cilia—"This cilia is tired of sweeping and has gone to sleep; this cilia is bigger than all the others and can sweep better," and so on. She was beaming; I was delighted and left her to draw all her cilia. Sometime later, her drawing changed to making "sillier" stick figures. "This is Mike being 'sillier' "; "This is how I look when I am 'sillier.' " By now, she was really having fun and turning out all kinds of stick figures with a droll sense of humor.

The other children were both envious and amused. Matilda was the center of attention and basked in being noticed. After that, she continued to draw stick figures and added all sorts of embellishments. When the group painted the mural, "The History of the World," Matilda was selected to draw in most of the figures. When we had a visitor's day for viewing the finished mural, Matilda's parents came. They were nearing sixty and were as quiet and unobtrusive as Matilda; they didn't say much in words, but their pleasure and pride were obvious when they saw Matilda's distinctive little figures in strategic areas of "The History of the World."

Matilda's reading improved somewhat as long as the material was related to something she could experience directly. She could learn new ideas best when we could find some way for her to contact the idea through her senses. Abstract data made no sense to Matilda, but her drawings did. Since she made them with her own hands, they were real to her; she could incorporate a lot of learning along with her visualizations.

My experiences with Matilda underlined what I had learned earlier—that my best way of teaching and doing therapy was to be as relaxed and aware and alert as possible, to receive cues from the children themselves. I forget this learning sometimes and impatiently try to fit individual people into theoretical boxes. When I do, the people and I are both uncomfortable with the results.

When this happens, I stop trying to control how I can fit the patient to a fact; I remember how Matilda's growth from an apparent nonentity into a personal identity began when she made contact with some little hairs called "sillier"; when I remember that, I know that I can't plan any controlled methods to rival the ones that can happen spontaneously in a real live relationship.

BRIDGING SOME GAPS

Interspersed with my chaotic days in the shabby little school where the kids and I battled with art materials and growing-up problems, I went to the rehabilitation center of a large naval hospital and served as an occupational therapist with men who were paraplegics. There, everything appeared to be completely organized, and everyone seemed to know exactly what role he was to play in the common goal of providing these men with something interesting to do while they learned to live with their psychic and physical wounds.

The large room was sunny and well-equipped; the men, dressed alike in blue pajamas and robes, were quietly respectful; the nurses were pleasant and helpful; and we all avoided recognizing the horror that these men were crippled beyond repair. At least, that's the way it seemed to me. I saw the men only a few hours a week, and it took me a while to catch on that most of them regarded art with awe and were actually embarrassed when I offered to help them do anything they wanted to with the art materials. Their diffident smiles and polite acquiescence to all my suggestions left me feeling frustrated. I wanted them to do something they wanted to do; they wanted me to tell them what I wanted them to do! We weren't getting anywhere until one large man in a wheelchair, with folded-back pajamas where his legs should have been, said with a scowl and a heavy voice, "Well, I know what I want to do. I want to make something pretty for my wife." That earnest statement introduced Cliff to me and broke the impasse of restraint between the materials and the men. None of them felt brave enough to attempt a free painting, and I didn't like the idea of their turning out repetitious mold-made objects, so we settled on textile painting. With yards of plain cloth, jars of bright colors, brushes, and a minimum of instruction, the men could paint according to their own tastes. Some made bold patterns, some brushed on timid floral designs; two men played tic-tac-toe with the paint on the cloth. The nurses ironed the lengths of material to make the colors wash-proof; the tic-tac-toe buddies had twin shirts made out of their material to wear when they would leave the hospital and go their separate ways.

I was glad for the men's playfulness with the materials; I was relieved that they had forgotten their awe of ART in making something that was both pleasing and useful; I was delighted that they laughed with each other at their efforts and errors.

Cliff

Nobody laughed at Cliff; this man was serious and dedicated to "making something pretty." He did, too. He made a complete set of place mats with napkins to match; he cut the cloth neatly, pulled threads to make fringes; and on each piece he painted apple blossoms —pink apple blossoms bursting out of dark wood boughs. It is not easy to do such delicate forms with brushes on rough cloth, but Cliff was steadily persistent with his gentle strokes. He never smiled. He was not a young man—his face was seamed with lines of pain—but when he finished the last mat and they had been neatly ironed, his eyes and the way his hands smoothed the cloth told of his satisfaction that he had made something worthy of giving to his wife.

Though I was satisfied with the way the men used the art materials, I never felt that I knew any of them as persons, except Cliff. I knew nothing about even Cliff's former or future life, but while he was in the art room, when we talked of how to paint springtime apple blossoms growing from twisted wood, I knew we were speaking of more than the design he was painting on a piece of cloth.

I also knew, even with Cliff, that we were avoiding speaking directly of the actuality that this strong man would never again stand on his own two feet. Perhaps it was wise not to talk of this cruel fact with me; I was there specifically to offer diversion; maybe Cliff and the other men had outlets somewhere else for expressing the dark reality of their losses. Still, I felt that we were all covering up and pretending a large part of the time.

Since I used art media to release my own anger and pain, as well as for creating playful forms, I would have felt better if some of the men at some time could have used the materials for expressing whatever blocked-up resentments I assumed they surely must be feeling. However, I never suggested this to them. I knew that my role in that vast hospital organization was set by men whom I never saw personally and whose policies I questioned but followed nonetheless.

In an elegant art center of a wealthy suburb where I held art classes on two evenings a week, I had the same uneasy feelings that we were avoiding, by implicit consent, anything that might threaten our pose that "God's in his heaven—all's right with the world." All wasn't right in my world—that I knew for sure. Also I knew many of my students personally, and some of them had messy private lives. But we did not speak openly to each other of our troubles. In the evening classes, men and women painted as an escape instead of as a way of getting in touch with what was real. Some even brought in picture postcards that they wanted to copy! I wanted to shout, "But art experience must come from you, not from a shiny little photograph!" But I didn't shout; in those days, I was still too polite. I diplomatically set up still life arrangements of vases, flowers, fruits, and gourds; I firmly insisted that if they didn't want to express their inner realities in art forms, they could paint their perception of some outside real things. I staunchly refused to help them copy someone else's painting.

The students enjoyed the sessions; some did satisfying paintings. The classes were successful in providing them with a way to express their own taste in composition, forms, and colors, and they congratulated each other. I was genuinely pleased and satisfied that I was contributing to a real need in this community center.

But my own needs were being stuffed down deeper under layers of pretense. I was an adequate art teacher and I could paint reasonably well, but I wanted more than that from the art experience. I wanted more for other people, too; I wanted them to know experientially that we could use art to get closer to reality. I didn't want them to be afraid of reality; mostly, I wanted to overcome my own fears of facing reality. But I was afraid of exposing myself, so I paced around smilingly encouraging while I felt like crying.

William

Then I noticed that one man never painted the still lifes I set up. I had met him socially and knew that he was a physicist; like me, he was in his mid-thirties, but now I noticed how emaciated and old he looked. I saw too that all of his paintings were colorful abstractions, with very little form—just clear colors blending, merging, and separating into flowing streams of light. He asked me how to apply glazes, told me in words what feelings he wanted to express. And then, almost apologetically, confided that he had terminal cancer and wanted to paint the essence of his acceptance of his life's termination in this world and of his faith that his life force was flowing into some other unknown dimension. His faith was his own, and I could not go with him into that except through his paintings; with his paintings as a bridge between us, we could speak without reserve. We spoke of life and death and fear and the reality of all of these; we also spoke of beauty and faith and hope.

With William, in those last few months of his life, I regained some of my faith in the human potential of accepting what must be accepted with courage and without bitterness. William's keen mind had been used in the field of research in biophysics; now, he was using art experience to create beautiful imagery of his spiritual explorations and discoveries.

His wife told me after his death he had painted at home for hours at a time, always storing the paintings away in a closet, never looking at them again, immediately becoming absorbed in doing another. She brought some of them for me to see; they varied only slightly from one to the other. All of them were serenely integrated.

To me, the content of William's paintings spoke of a reality that few of us can experience—calm, almost impersonal acceptance. Though his physical body was disintegrating rapidly, he used his organic capacities, and perhaps some others we don't know much about, to preserve in concrete physical form a series of paintings that recorded his reconciliation of life and death. To me, his color-and-light paintings represented a transcendent reality. I was grateful that I had been able to assist him in using art media for himself.

My gratitude to William for what I learned from him was difficult for me to put into words. How could I say to a dying man, "You are teaching me a great deal about how to live"? How could I say, "In this room full of people noisily intent on vying with each other for scintillating sophistication in their words and with their clever productions, only your quiet voice and your uncluttered paintings enliven me." Perhaps William knew, though, what I wanted to say and understood that his presence quieted the petty resentments and irritations on which I was spending so much time and energy.

William didn't waste his limited time and energy; he was living each hour while he was painting, seemingly so absorbed in what he was doing that he seemed oblivious to the clutter and chatter in the room. I think he had reached a state of being in which he was conserving his waning physical energy so he could discover how much he could express what Frank Barron calls psychological vitality. Through William's frail body emerged the triumphant energy with which he synthesized in color, clearly and vividly, both his process and his philosophy; I do not mean to say that the paintings in themselves were great works of art or that William professed to any great all-encompassing philosophy of truth; I do mean to say that he expressed his ceasing to strive for the worldly things we were all making such a fuss about acquiring; he did so with composure, not avoiding his reality but not imposing it on anyone else either.

Frank Barron describes the emotional and mental state that I believe William had reached:

When such simplicity amid complexity has been achieved, I think that two new and most important effects come into existence in the individual's experience. One of these is the feeling that one is free and that life and its outcome are in one's own hands. The other is a new experience of the passage of time and a deeper sense of relaxed participation in the present moment. All of experience is consequently permanent at the very moment of its occurrence, and life ceases to be a course between birth and death and becomes instead a fully realized experience of change in which every single state is as valid and as necessary as every other.[1]

BOTH/AND

"Every single state is as valid . . . as every other," says Frank Barron. When I am feeling at one with myself, I accept that truth for me and for others. But I prefer some states to others; in the years since I held classes in art, I have followed my preferences and made choices for the way I want to live. My personal choices often affect the lives of others—sometimes they have opposed my choices and sometimes I have opposed theirs. Inevitably, we can't always come to a pleasant agreement.

In my vocation, centered in art, I have learned much from that dear teacher, experience. Foolishly or not, I have chosen to shift my orientations and acting outs from one area to another. I have not walked a straight and narrow path from there to here; from my teaching art to others, I learned how much I needed to be taught; from my years of living in expatriate artist colonies, I learned how much I wanted to live with all sorts of people; from my years of living in intentional communities, I found out that I wanted more time to be alone; from giving up close contact with art and people, I knew that I needed to come back into the stimulating, exasperating, and challenging sphere of relationships with others through art experience. So, zigging and zagging, plodding down some paths that led nowhere and meandering onto some others that widened into vistas, I covered a lot of territory. I grew from the tender young chick who thought, "There must be a way to make life-stories have happy endings; if I could just find the way!" to the tough old bird I am now who thinks, "Yeah! There are many ways of living fully if we can accept them as parts of a whole configuration instead of single states complete in themselves."

I'm still exploring; still burning bridges and building rafts; still a "person in process" like some others whose explorations are pre-

Frank Barron, *Creativity and Personal Freedom,* rev. ed. (New York: Van Nostrand Reinhold, 1968), pp. 5-6.

sented in later chapters. I hope I will continue this process of always being on the lookout for more complete answers for many years yet; I hope I can remain in the company of other people who experiment and risk, who sometimes get themselves into muddles in the interest of finding innovative ways of being more fully functioning humans. I need and welcome these companions because I am refusing to grow old gracefully and refusing to accept conformist standards, which I find inhibiting to personal growth—mine and other people's. In my stubborn crusade I sometimes can't distinguish between windmills and dragons and I sometimes get myself into ludicrous situations.

Right now, my zeal is directed toward tilting with what I consider a real dragon in the practice of using art therapeutically. I call this dragon the "either/or syndrome"; I see it blocking a road that could lead us to a truly useful avenue of using the large variety of art media more effectively if we can slay that tough-skinned creature who bellows uncompromisingly, "either this or that: *either* therapy *or* education *or* personal growth" as if any of these acts and goals and values could be separated one from the other! Art experience is for personal growth, *and* for education, *and* for increasing awareness *and* perceptiveness *and* creativity *and* a sense of personal identity, *and* for much more— *and* all of these are intrinsic parts of the whole therapeutic process.

The whole therapeutic process is endangered by the either/or division of the participants into either sick or well categories; the therapist who sits complacently and views the art expressions of his patients only as symptomatic of this or that hyphenated classification of neurosis or psychosis is feeding the either/or dragon beefsteaks for breakfast!

I know many therapists; I know many diagnostic terms, and I can apply them to people with a fair percentage of accuracy. I know myself, I see my art work; if I didn't know me—if I saw my drawings with cold, diagnostic eyes—I could condemn me with some chilling psychopathological prognoses!

Fortunately, many therapists are unintimidated by the either/or dragon; we can accept ourselves and those for whom we are therapists as being, all of us, people in process. In different phases of process, surely. Some of us need more assistance than others; all of us have times when we are not functioning fully; none of us is invulnerable; none of us is free from fear and insecurity. So we learn, support, challenge, and grow together.

We do not dehumanize each other by denying our common humanity. We know that we all view ourselves, each other, and our world through individual eyes; we perceive subjectively as well as objectively. Only computers can be totally objective; persons who deny their subjectivity are playing the dangerous game of "make believe I'm a know-it-all robot. All you have to do is push the right button, and I'll give you the right answer."

The either/or dragon is a robot construction; he can be dismantled and reduced to powerlessness if we, person to person, can accept all of us as being in different places on the road of discovery and recognize that we can all learn some new directions from each other.

In the art experience, especially, the creator of the forms perceives and expresses far more subtle nuances than can ever be fitted into theoretically classified tight little boxes.

Specifically, in my contact and communication with the persons who have shared their art forms with me, I have received insights that assist me in my own art and work. Bob's patience, Mike's energy, Matilda's humility, Cliff's courage, and William's quiet acceptance were their individual personal qualities with which I could connect in facilitating their search for themselves and mine for myself.

Each did his own work, and I did mine; each was willing to express his inner needs, and I was willing to accept what he showed me as being a valid message from his unique personality. In order for us to find constructive therapeutic paths, both they and I had to invest ourselves in the process.

I refer back to the private school situation of years ago because it was there that I learned how art could be used therapeutically when the concept of either/or was thrown out completely in favor of the viable both/and concept. Of necessity, I was both teacher and therapist for the kids; conversely, several of them were both teacher and therapist for me. In the process we all learned a good bit.

That learning has served me well. Now, when I am menaced by the either/or syndrome, I take time out to apply both/and. Usually, I can find my way through seemingly impossible dichotomies.

I am both teacher and therapist in the gestalt art experience. When I am with someone in this dual role, I am both leader and follower; the person with whom I am working is both my guide and is guided by me. Most important, both the other person and I must seek and honor the uniqueness of each of us. I follow my conviction that each of us is expressing both weakness and strength—both needs and resources. In my interpretation of the client's art, I am convinced that I must see it both through my perception and, as much as possible, empathize with the patient's perception. I must trust that the creator of the art form is potentially capable of self-interpretation that is more complete than my interpretation of his personality. Sometimes the patient is not aware of his own potential, so I must rely on my own interpretation. Sometimes I do not empathize with the patient and so do not trust my perceptions. Mostly, though, when a patient and I are both seeking together, we can discover not only the negativity revealed in the art forms but also some awareness of what is potentially positive.

Now, when people come to me for therapeutic art experience, whether they are sent by their psychotherapists or come on their own,

I usually feel relaxed and confident that I can offer media and methods to help them get in touch with their own needs and with ways of finding their own answers. Sometimes it doesn't work out so directly; then, both the client and I must explore all sorts of approaches and alternate media. When we face the challenge head on and together, this is an exciting and growth-producing experience for both of us.

At times I have worked with someone who could not or would not cooperate with what I suggested, nor had he any constructive ideas of his own. In those situations, I put aside my training as a gestalt art therapist and draw on all my life's learning. Investing myself as a total person into a struggle with another, as a total person, usually brings about some sort of positive response, but there have been times when I have emerged from the battle frayed around the edges and without any certainty that my unorthodox behavior has benefited the patient.

Penny

My work with Penny, which took place three years ago and lasted several months, was highly unorthodox. Though I think I helped her recover from a severe psychotic phase, I cannot be sure how and to what extent because there were so many complications other than those she and I dealt with directly in her art therapy.

Her doctor contacted me at Penny's request and told me of the situation and its urgency; Penny was 17 years old and seemed determined to die. A year before she had taken LSD for the first time and while under its influence had quietly stepped into empty space from the roof of a building. Now, after months in a hospital, she was confined to a wheelchair and to living with her desperate parents. They blamed the LSD and Penny's friends at the university where she had been an art student; they were determined to keep Penny at home, and Penny was equally determined to be independent even though she knew she could never walk again. I talked with her doctor and two of the half dozen psychotherapists who were called on when Penny would commit other self-destructive acts. They supported my opinion that far more was involved than the drug effect and that Penny's desire for using art therapy was possibly one way to help her. At least it was worth trying.

For several months, in the midst of all sorts of unpredictable crises, Penny and I met four hours weekly in private sessions. I provided the art materials and she accepted them greedily, but she never used them in my presence, and she would not let me see any of the art she had done privately until after she had reduced it to debris. She said that she made drawings and tore them to bits, and that she didn't like working with ceramic clay because it hardened and was difficult for her to destroy. I bought pounds of plasticene, which Penny could squeeze into ever-changing shapes while she talked to me. Her hand move-

ments were as frenetic as her stream-of-consciousness talk of her plans
to become a self-supporting artist when she either became legally of
age or could persuade her parents to allow her to live away from home.
It was increasingly obvious that Penny needed much more than separation from her parents, though that was accomplished when she injured
herself again and required hospitalization, which was followed by a long
period of in-patient therapy and eventually by her returning to art
school.

Penny needed more than art therapy, too, which I realized
soon after I began seeing her. What I could offer was a sort of stop-gap
measure to give her some outlet for her destructive energy. While she
spoke rationally to me of her plans for constructive action, her acting-
out with art media was to create forms in order to destroy them. I don't
think that Penny knew consciously what she was doing, but I am convinced that she was using the art materials both as catharsis and as a
way of experiencing directly her need to destroy all of the restraints that
kept her from getting what she wanted.

I find this kind of destructive use of art materials very valuable
for others who are much less disturbed than Penny. They can use the
media consciously, often humorously, to create effigies of their enemies
and then destroy them with fiendish glee. Voodoo artists are said to
bring about actual death to others. I don't encourage voodoo magic in
art experience sessions (who knows—it might actually work!), but I do
encourage people who are full of frustrated anger at themselves, at
others, and at the world in general to vent their rage on materials
instead of on people.

Of course, this kind of emotional explosion should be allowed
only when the person involved is stable enough to be able to discriminate between "I'm squashing my clay wife-image in fantasy" and "I'm
going to smash my real wife at home." No one has ever done violence to
any other person in my studio; as far as I know, no one has left with that
intent. Nonetheless, if I am in doubt about someone's ability to determine his own limits of acting out, I tend to close the dampers and slow
the fire down a bit until I am surer that we know just how much heat the
stove can throw out without blowing up.

When I write "that *we* know," I intend the "we" to mean "the
patient-client-participant and I." Art media must be used by each person as his own needs define if the art experience is to be a valid factor
for positive growth in education, rehabilitation, and therapy. Also, I am
convinced that my greatest contribution to the process of being teacher
and therapist with another person is in receiving that person as a unique
individual living his reality in a way that he has chosen in response to
the problems and patterns inherent in his own highly individualized
situation.

My response-ability to each person, then, is the best asset I can bring to any relationship. I can adapt the art media and generalized methods of using the materials to the individual best when I am guided by his reality needs; in order to do this, the art experience must be an I-thou relationship, including the client as an active agent in knowing, on some awareness level, what he needs. My part in the therapeutic relationship is to facilitate the awareness of the participant so that he can then find the best possible way to work for personal growth through art media.

People sometimes choose strange ways: Bob's tight mouth and drawings, Mike's wild splashings, Matilda's "sillier" figures, Cliff's pretty apple blossoms, William's color and light mergings, and Penny's create-and-destroy forms were all individually chosen ways of expressing their needs and efforts toward fulfilling them. In each case, the person found a way that seemed best for his personality at that time and that place.

So, what is strange to one person is natural to another, and when each of us can recognize the other's way as being a genuine expression of a whole complex personality, both of us can grow and learn, become more aware, and discover ways of actualizing unique human potentials far beyond the boundaries that we impose on ourselves and each other when we are caught in the throes of fear-ridden fantasies.

WE AND THEY

One of the areas in which both fantasy and actuality get all mixed up in a frustrating and sometimes terrifying composite reality is the conflict between establishment parents and hippie children. I became involved in this scene some years ago and still often find myself in an intermediary role between the generations. At one time I felt as if I were a wizened little pigmy standing in the middle of that uninhabited gap, reaching out skinny arms a mile long toward the wild-haired young with one hand and the carefully barbered middle-aged with the other. In my fantasy, my voice cracked and creaked as I implored, "Come on, fellows! Stop paying so much attention to your hairstyles and attend to both your real differences and your real communalities!" My words croaked because I was both laughing and crying.

That I was alone in that much-publicized gap was my self-delusion; lots of people, from many ages and culture groups, are in that space between. Though popular literature presents an either/or picture lumping radical youth on one side and a cluster of conservative elders on the other with a no-man's land between, that presentation is much too simplistic. I think that many people, both conservative and radical, prefer to accept that picture because it gives them an excuse to avoid stretching their perceptions to realize that they are actually taking part in a complex motion picture for which no script has been provided. We are all in this together; we are writing our own lives, we are directing our individual acts, and we are doing this in a field that has no space for a gap or a neutral no-man's land.

During 1966 and 1967 I lived in the Haight-Ashbury in a four-story, gingerbreaded Victorian house. Three of us leased the house, having in mind lots of space for painting studios and fantasies of long, quiet evenings spent in private musings in front of soft glows from the tiny fireplaces, with the white plaster cherubs in the ceiling decorations reminding us of gracious, leisurely living. Well, it didn't work out that way; we had not foreseen the "summer of love" and the "flower children" who would come not only up to our doorstep but all the way up the stairs and into my fourth-floor studio. Up those four flights came drugs, tear gas, hippies, helpers, militants, ministers, messiahs, therapists, freaked-out kids, and bearded and beaded 20-year-old solid citizens, soberly taking responsibility for bringing whatever order they could into the colorful but mind-bending chaos.

Before this phenomenon, the art experience groups in my studio had not been monotonously predictable, but there had been patterns of consistency we could rely on. The participants were mostly middle-class, middle-aged Caucasians who shared some taken-for-granted values. When Haight and Ashbury became not just streets but the center of an unprecedented social experiment, the art experience groups became something else again. Different kinds of people came—very different kinds of people. In one group a dozen or so would be sitting in a circle, creating their individual art forms and sharing their thoughts and feelings openly with each other. A 60-year-old man working with the National Institute of Mental Health on the problem of drug abuse sat cross-legged on a paint-smeared floor. He interpreted his painting to a 16-year-old girl draped in a window-curtain sari and glistening with perfumed oil, who listened earnestly to the older man, then spoke of her own psychedelic drawings. An 18-year-old boy, dark hair curling on his shoulders, encouraged a 72-year-old matron to take off her shoes and move her body with the rhythm of her paint brush; he held her hand and both of them giggled when she discovered she could synchronize her toes with his.

All sorts of unlikely things happened to the unlikely people who came to the groups; often people who could barely understand each other's vocabularies painted together on the same roll of paper. What they painted was not necessarily all cooperative sweetness and light—in fact, many sheets of paper were torn furiously in half and sometimes a hunk of clay got plastered against the wall by a frustrated participant who fortunately chose to demolish a clay figure instead of a person! Sometimes the symbolic destructions served as outlets for violence so that afterwards the persons involved could settle down to some face-to-face communicating, paying attention to each other and listening with caring concentration.

To my glad surprise, some parents came with their teen-agers and used art media to reveal themselves to each other. Since I empathized with both, I could often assist them to at least see the other as a separate person rather than as a projection of their own false fantasies. I think, too, that some of the parent-child pairs began to see deeper into the individuality of the other and could then interchange ideas that were truly their own instead of batting clichés back and forth.

I ponder the benefits of those art experiences: "What happened?" I ask myself. I honestly don't know how far-reaching the effects were; I do know that quite a few people contacted one another in a way that forced them to recognize the genuine differences between flesh-and-blood persons and the stereotyped aliens they were supposed to be. I know that some of those flower children had never before seen an honest-to-God psychotherapist. When they did in the art sessions, they were amazed that he was not an ogre. He, in turn, was surprised at how compelling a wisp of a girl could be in telling him why she chose to live in a hippie commune. And then there was the beautifully coiffed Jungian analyst who was terrified of the black teen-ager from the Mission District until she discovered how similarly they both expressed their feelings of loneliness in imagery.

No matter what else happened, quite a few of us found it increasingly difficult to divide people into the good guys and the bad guys. In those confusing sessions, the gaps between generations, races, life-styles, and status didn't seem nearly so important; the dividing line between who is "we" and who is "they" became increasingly difficult to draw.

"The Boy"

Figure 4 and the protest poem that accompanies it were done by someone who I think of as "the boy": 17 years old, accused of possessing marijuana, arrested with a group of much older people by a narcotics agent who planted the dope, the boy, in despair, took an overdose of sleeping pills. Recovering and in the care of a psychotherapist, he bitterly resented being told by his lawyer that he must cut his long hair and wear conventional clothes to appear in court in order to receive a fair hearing from the conservative judge.

The boy cut his hair, behaved as he was required to, spoke politely in court, and the charges against him were dismissed. Meanwhile, he withdrew from family, friends, and a society he regarded only as an enemy; he drew pictures and wrote in solitude. He passed his own judgments on those who judged him not for his guilt or innocence as a drug user but for his choice of hair style and clothes. There are many such boys and girls, wandering and wondering and wanting to be heard by someone who cares enough to listen when they ask for an honest open hearing.

Figure 4. "The Boy."

Figure 4 was his first drawing; he brought it and the poem to me when he heard that I was interested in seeing it and listening to him as he was perceiving himself to be. He said that the figure is a self-portrait of his inside feeling-self, his self-imagery. Here is his poem:

My hands are stained with blood, my blood; and you try to wash them, to replace them. I am only learning, and I will continue, if I can, once you're through.

I am disgusted by your world and the thought of my soul, bargaining, at your mercy.

I am disgusted by your wonder that my hands are soft and my voice is calm.

I am disgusted at your judgment and judgments to come and judgments that have passed and the ones that destroy all worlds except your perilous, mechanical wheel . . . the fool.

Fortunately, his parents were good people who wanted to understand and support their bewildering son. He is now in college, studying art and finding friends among his peers.

LIFE-STREAMS

I like to think of each person's life process as being like a stream that begins in some secret place and wends its way to some yet unknown sea.

When I am in a plane, I can look down and see the patterns of streams and rivers. Some make curlicue windings; others go straight ahead; some are dammed up; some seep into stagnant marshes; some seem to disappear; and sometimes I see waters that are flooding out of control.

From up there in the sky, I am inclined toward philosophical metaphors. I muse, "Yes, that's the way our lives flow. Our life-streams are carrying each of us along a channel formed by our human natures moving in our environments."

This metaphor still seems valid when I am down on earth again, but I cannot maintain the cool detachment from human life-streams that I feel when I am thousands of feet up in the air. Down here I am involved in day-to-day human reality, aware of my own humanness, concerned with daily direct contacts that keep me from flying high into the stratosphere of cosmic insights or plunging into the depths of all-knowing earthiness.

I know that my environmental background has influenced my comparison of the flow of a river and the life-stream of a person.

I was born and raised in northwest Florida. In a radius of 100 miles or so, many different natural and social elements converge and commingle. The foothills of the Blue Ridge Mountains meander down to the Gulf Coast; the Okefenokee Swamp spreads between the hills; rivers red with clay or pale green with limestone meet and merge on their way to the Gulf. They wander and sink beneath the hills and swamps into the intricate maze of limestone caves and then flow to the surface again in unexpected rushes. From some of them, the clearest water imaginable bubbles out, forming sparkling lakes. Diving into these blue holes was a favorite sport. The challenge was swimming against the spring's upward thrust, going as deep as possible into the mouth of the cave. A few times when I was in my teens, I had the courage and the tenacity to dive deep, grab hold of the underground rocks, and pull myself into the dark caverns below. I remember vividly how excited and frightened I was; how daring I felt exploring the hidden source of the spring, opposing its force, yet trusting it to push me out and up into the sunlight again. As soon as I released my hold on the rocks, I was carried immediately with the water's powerful flow so quickly that my head bobbed up above the surface of the lake like a bubble from the spring. My exhilaration at thrusting into the bright air was as great as the breathless ecstasy of plunging into the twilight water, exploring for myself the mysteries that lay below.

The blue holes that I knew have remained constant in their flow, sending forth about the same quantity of water year after year, keeping the lake fresh and clean, and pushing a stream down through the woods. However, I have heard awesome tales that they are not always to be trusted to flow consistently. In my grandfather's time, I am told, my favorite blue spring suddenly reversed its flow. Instead of gushing out, the water rushed back into the earth and disappeared, leaving a half-dried mud flat where once there had been a lake. How long this lasted I don't know, but the story goes that the spring started sending out its water again as suddenly and mysteriously as it had sucked it in.

I have seen rivers and creeks go underground. I have followed the course of a river 50 feet wide and have seen where it simply disappears. The water's course may go underground for one-half mile and then emerge again.

A clear, coffee-colored creek that I played in as a child rippled over sand quite serenely for most of its length, but at one place it flowed into a dark pool, circled slowly, and sank out of sight. A few hundred feet away the creek emerged in a swampy bog and continued flowing in the same general direction it had been pursuing. This puzzled and intrigued me. I would look into the somber pool, throw some object into it, and then walk over to the bog to see if I could see the object come out after its journey underground. I never had the satisfaction of finding out for sure that it was the same water coming up that went down, but I accepted the explanation that water, taking the path of least resistance, will flow in the channel nature provides. In our part of the country, the natural course for the streams often was to go under earth barriers instead of around them. It was easier that way.

In retrospect, I know that I identify strongly with those caves and underground streams. I was shy and introverted, hiding my anger, fear, and loneliness even from myself. As the oldest child in a large family, I assumed an adult role and suppressed many of my emotional needs. I became very adept in keeping secret my feelings of hurt and helplessness, especially with other girls in social situations. Like the streams, when I came to a barrier too big to go around and too high to wear down, I went underground into my dark, subterranean level. I still do, but now I am far more aware of what I am doing and conscious that I choose to withdraw into my inner world. Mostly now I flow along in my chosen course, not letting too much of me go underground for too long. Having a fairly reliable feeling for the terrain, I can wander through dark, intricate passageways without being fearful of losing my path back into the light. I know what I feel, though, when I am so confused by the cavern walls that I don't know in what direction I am moving or if I am moving at all. When I'm lost so deep in the dark that I can't see myself or feel myself as being me, then I'm terrified and need help.

Clarice

In the living process, some of our ground supports cave in and our vitality sinks underground, getting lost in dark labyrinths; a way back up into air and light is not easy to find. Sometimes the art experience brings out into the open vital energies that have been long submerged. This was true for Clarice.

When I agreed to spend some time with Clarice in private art experience sessions, I had no idea how to begin to help her. Her therapist had no suggestions to offer, either, except one warning: "Clarice is in both private and group therapy and can function fairly well until she is physically touched by another person; do what you think best with the art materials, but remember, she can't stand to be touched!"

I had to restrain myself often in my hours with Clarice since I do a lot of getting in touch with others physically without consciously thinking about it. The evening before our first private session, I sat in a group with Clarice, seeing how she leaned away from others, her face completely expressionless, her hands resting on the chair arms like dead things, her feet apart and unmoving on the floor.

I perceived, "Clarice tries not to touch herself." I assumed, "Sensually and emotionally she's gone underground." I puzzled, "How can I offer art experiences that go deep enough to reach her when she is so frightened of any kind of contact with living processes?"

The next morning in the studio, Clarice stood like a pale, forlorn young zombie, her whole body quiet but taut while her eyes darted about the room, registering dismay at the array of materials—clay, paint, chalk, glue, scissors, rough paper rolls—all media for stimulating tactile sensations. "Poor kid," I thought, "Which medium will be the least terrifying for her? How to begin?"

Clarice noticed a glass jar full of tiny pebbles I had collected from the beach. "Those look pretty," she said in her small, thin voice. "Would you like to look at them more closely?" I questioned in my least persuasive tone. She answered, "Yes," and thus, warily, we made a tentative beginning.

I put a very white, clean, smooth sheet of paper on a table and poured the pebbles on it. Clarice sat stiffly in a straight chair and looked at the random pattern of the darkish pebbles on the paper. I went on with another project, making some small montages by dipping pieces of wet seaweed into white glue and letting them dry in their natural shapes on white granular-surfaced paper. I was enjoying what

I was doing, but I was concentrating with peripheral vision on what Clarice was doing. For a while she made no outward movements at all. I noticed again that she held the parts of her body as separate from each other as she possibly could. She did not fold her hands or put them in her lap or on her legs; nor did she cross her legs or arms. "Dismembered, untouchable," I thought. How can she find release from that taboo?"

Then with the thumb and middle finger of each hand, she very delicately lifted the edges of the paper and shook it gently so that the pebbles would roll around into different patterns. After a few such experiments, Clarice began picking up the pebbles and dropping them, watching how they arranged themselves as they hit the paper. Finally, she began arranging them into designs of her own preference and calling my attention to those she liked, even interpreting to me what she saw in the configurations. The first designs were described as "stars in the sky" and "flowers in a field."

There came an hour when Clarice worked very intently, choosing pebbles for size, shape, and color. Trying out all kinds of relationships, she got a sheet of cardboard and expanded the size of her mosaic. Without her usual timidity she took some larger colored stones from other jars and created a group of figures that obviously belonged together.

Then she announced triumphantly, "There! That's exactly the way I want it! That's me and all the people I know put together! Now, I want to glue them down like you did the seaweed." In my consternation, I spluttered, "But the seaweed had glue on it before I put it down; your pebbles are dry and the board is dry and you can't. . . ." She started to cry: "But I want to stick all the stones and pebbles together just the way they are right now!" This was important for Clarice—crucially, terribly, beautifully important. So I gave her a little plastic squeeze bottle of white glue and showed her how to lift up each little pebble, squeeze a dollop of glue onto its bottom, and then press it back into place. She tried, but the glue got all over her hands, the pebbles stuck to her fingers, and finally she asked for help. I violated my rule of never doing anyone else's art work for him; obviously this was an emergency. That mosaic *had* to stick together! So Clarice and I worked together; sometimes her hands and mine would be literally stuck together with drying glue. We got glue on our faces and in our hair; we wiped the smears off each other and stuck down yet another pebble. We'd tilt the cardboard to see if we'd missed any stone; if one rolled, we'd grab it quickly and plunk it down into a white puddle. There must have been at least 100 little pebbles, but we got them all securely in place, and as the mosaic dried, we both carried it triumphantly from the studio to show to the therapist. She was amazed, not so much at the mosaic, but that Clarice and I were arm in arm, body to body, *touching.* We had forgotten all about that taboo!

Clarice returned to her home on the East Coast soon after that to live with her parents and go back into the psychotherapy she'd resisted by leaving home. She took her mosaic with her; I hope her pebbles will stick together in whatever touching relationship is best for her.

George

When George shambled into my studio, he told me that his life-force was so completely dammed that all his thoughts were of suicide as the only possible relief from the tremendous emotional pressure he was feeling—and, he said, he lacked the energy to do even that! He had little hope that the art experience suggested by his psychotherapist would be effective, but he was willing to give one last weary try to ease his unbearable stress of containing violent emotions he could not express.

George is a psychiatric social worker in his late fifties who had spent 20 years as a counselor for patients in mental institutions. His approach had always been nondirective, stressing love, faith, spirituality, and nonviolence. Through difficult personal times, he had sustained himself by giving extra time and energy to organizations pushing for social reform; he had, at the same time, denied himself as a needful human being. Then he had to face an ugly, incomprehensible family tragedy that seemed to make a mockery of all that he had believed in and worked for: his own son became so violently anti-social that he was legally confined to a correctional institution. Essentially an idealistic man, George simply didn't know how to face the raw, stark reality of his disillusionment. So he had built a wall, damming off his feelings because, he explained, he was afraid he would not be able to help others if he let himself experience his bitterness; after a few weeks of pretending lightheartedness while he was feeling heavy with sorrow, he found to his dismay that the patients who came to his office were becoming nonentities to him: he didn't perceive what they were saying; he didn't care what they said; he was irritated by their problems; he blamed the patients for their impotencies. Finally, he was aware of his thinly disguised disgust and antagonism toward all those who asked his help.

George was a conscientious man; he took a leave of absence and entered psychotherapy. There he was able to verbalize, rationalize, and analyze his repressed anger and resentment, but he couldn't feel or act out any negative emotions; he was emotionally immobilized.

So there he stood in my studio, standing in front of the large sheets of paper I'd laid out when he'd said, "All I know is that I feel like painting something big." Psychically immobilized, he stared with a baffled look that seemed to say, "How can I, meek and mild George, desecrate all that pristine paper to express the muck that is inside me?" I used a ploy that is often effective with self-controlled people like George; I grabbed the paper, wet it thoroughly, crumpled it up, and then spread it out again, all dripping and criss-crossed with cracks and creases. "Now the paper is already messed up; you don't have to be careful of ruining it or worry that you have to do something good. You can't do anything nice on such a raggedy surface, so don't try. Just put some paint on it and let happen what will!"

Things happened. George chose black and red paint; he brushed it on the wet paper, and the colors smeared and blurred. Then he began pouring the paint from the jars to make spreading pools of black mingling with red. He took more sheets of paper, twisting them, tearing them, and then painting around the gashes. He talked of "blood and guts," and spoke about "horror, terror, fury, nothingness." George recognized what was happening; no explanations were necessary. He just kept on painting, pounding some of the messy colored sheets into shapeless masses, throwing them into the trash basket, and then going on to another outburst with an ever-widening choice of colors and an ever-diminishing randomness. I left him alone; he painted for six hours. Months afterward he told me, "I expressed more of myself in that one day of painting than I had in a year of talking about myself in words."

George had opened the floodgates of his own dam and had safely released the powerful force that was destructive only as long as it was too contained. He joined an ongoing group and continued to tell about himself in paintings and more and more with words, too. Now that he was free to be himself, George had a lot to communicate. He became quite voluble with paintings, doing several in each session, using vibrant colors as his voice came alive with excitement. He was fascinated with a desert landscape theme, with sand, sky, and huge spiny cactus forms that dominated his paintings. He did a series of plants growing on earth backgrounds. Gradually the plants became more alive and semi-abstract. Palm fronds appeared instead of stark Judas trees.

Along with the changes in his painting, George changed in his attitude toward others in the group. He spoke without apologizing in every sentence; he spoke for himself, getting out of the compulsive helper role, and was able to allow his sadness free flow without being afraid that he would depress someone else. Thus he could even allow someone else to support him when he was feeling need for that.

George remained a gentle person. He did not repeat his one wild orgy of "blood and guts" kind of painting. He returned to his work in the mental hospital, and when I talked with him recently he said, with a rueful smile, "Yes, I'm doing fine—not perfect, some ups and downs like everybody else; but all in all, I'm doing fine."

Tony

I find that the gestalt art experience is a natural outlet for people whose life energies have gone underground, like Clarice's, or when their forcefulness is dammed up, as George's was; but when someone's vitality has just spread out and seeped into a stagnant marsh-like ennui, I feel at a loss in knowing what kind of art experiences can help to motivate some kind of flow so that the person can get out of his morass of chronic boredom.

For instance, there is Tony; for years now, he has been coming to the art experience groups sporadically. He has no great problems to solve; no dramatic crises occur in his life; in fact, nothing much happens to get his juices flowing. He has a fairly good job; he functions adequately; he has reasonably satisfying relationships with women; he gets along. But that is all he does! He's getting along in years, too; at 40, he has not married, has not realized his vague aspirations of becoming a recognized professional artist; everything he has done thus far in his life has been half-hearted. His participation in the art groups is half-hearted, too; he lethargically draws pictures of other people, asks questions about their feeling-responses, but says little about himself either in art, words, or actions—except that I've noticed that Tony actually goes to sleep whenever the group's attention seems to be turning toward him as a personality. I conclude that Tony both does and does not want to move in any direction that might ruffle his shallow, undefined, but comfortably unthreatening way of life.

At times I have been tempted to throw some sort of psychic dynamite into his lackadaisical marsh in hopes of blasting out a drainage ditch for him to move into, but I don't do that. Tony chooses his own course, and neither the art experience nor group interaction nor I can find a channel for him. Tony will have to take responsibility for stirring himself if he truly wants to find a way out of his drowsiness. If he snores once more during a group project, though, I am likely to forget my professional ethics and clout him with a hunk of clay!

Kathy

For persons who are in a flood stage of receiving more stimulations and excitements than they can contain, the art experience offers an immediate medium for cathartic expression; often high-keyed people need no more than a time and place to overflow in a permissive atmosphere where their vociferousness is not looked upon as madness. After these wild expressions are out on paper, their creator relaxes and wants long, quiet, assimilating, and integrating discussions. This may take time; weeks of repeated letting go alternating with periods of clear recognition of what boundaries are appropriate for life situations.

Kathy was a social worker who specialized in being with teen-agers while they were on drugs; she was especially perceptive with kids on "bum trips"; with them she was calm, supportive, attentive, and reassuring. But the price she paid for her assumed serenity was to sup-press her own rush of emotions, figuratively sandbagging the flood of fears, futility, anger, hope, and challenge that engulfed her.

So, once a week, she came to my studio with the openly stated need to let her pent-up exasperations overflow with paint. And that she did!

Streams of colors ran over the floor from the large sheets of muslin she pinned on a wall and attacked with loaded brushes. After-ward, she would lie on the couch and breathe deeply and regularly, exhausted but again willing and able to direct the steady flow of her energy in her chosen channel.

Kathy did not need to talk about what she had done with the paint; she knew how to open her own flood-gates, and she could close them and bear the pressure when she had to. George needed to let his emotions show in some way, but he was terrified that he would drown in his own flood if he released his feelings totally. The art media allowed him to express non-verbally what he would not put into words. He learned experientially what Kathy took for granted—that he needed an outlet for emotions too diffuse for logical words and, more important, that he was capable of directing those emotions constructively.

Clarice needed help in directing her life-stream; she had not yet found any flow that was her own. Putting the pebbles together let her see that she could touch some desire that was hers and allowed her to accept my touch without fear. Then she went back with more hope to work in psychotherapy toward designing some direction of her own.

For most of the people I write about in this chapter, the art experience was something they turned to in a time of crisis. For each one the experience was different—as different as were their needs; they used the art media in individual ways that were congruent with their own processes of growth.

Helen, "Monster Man."

Helen, "Moods."

PLATE 1

Norman, "Tough Old Tree."

Norman, "Accusing Eye."

Cyndy, "I Want."

PLATE 2

Cyndy, "Perhaps Tomorrow."

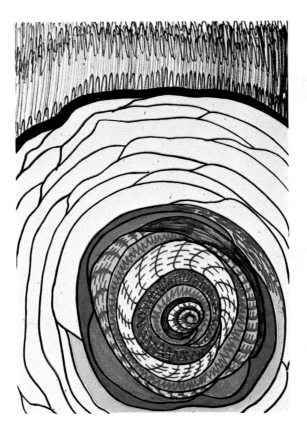

Celia, "Inside Myself."

PLATE 3

Celia, "All Over the Place."

Coeleen, "Little Black Boy."

Coeleen, "Stretched Out on the Beach."

PLATE 4

Chapter Three

GROWING WITH ART EXPERIENCE

USING FANTASY TO FIND REALITY

In his marvelously rich, compact little book, *A Catalog of the Ways People Grow,* Severin Peterson said:

Each person is his own way of growth.
This is basic.
The persons and processes listed in this book are
    auxiliaries.
It can happen that these ways can interfere with one's own
    way.
Mainly, though, they can help a lot, if you use them in the
    right way, your way.

If the teacher of a way is respected, you will respect him.
If the teacher of a way gives you his best, you will give him
    your best.
If a way becomes bigger than you, you have either made a
    wonderful discovery or an enormous mistake.

Severin Peterson, *A Catalog of the Ways People Grow* (New York: Ballantine, 1971).

In the preceding chapter I told you about some people whose ways of growth had become too big or maybe too small for them; I told you also of some who didn't even know how to seek a way for themselves. Most of them were in trouble; their life-patterns created problems that kept them from functioning adequately. Getting out of trouble was their priority need, and we channeled their energies in that direction when we worked together.

Other people do not seem to be in trouble; they can and do cope with life's problems adequately, even admirably; then they turn up at growth centers, in workshops, in group dynamics meetings saying, "I'm doing all right. I don't need a therapist, but I want something. I need something more—I want to grow into being more than I am."

These people are self-motivated, self-directed, and they choose their own kinds of teachers. Some of them come to me wanting to try the gestalt art experience to facilitate their personal growth. This chapter describes some of these people in their process of personal growth.

Fantasy is a large part of my work with people in process. I value using fantasy as a way of expanding and exploring personalities, and I encourage people to fantasize creatively, taking their chances at finding wonderful as well as not so wonderful realizations.

Part of my introduction to fantasy as one way of finding reality comes from Fritz Perls, who writes: ". . . there is a big area of fantasy activity that takes up so much of our excitement, of our energy, of our life force, that there is very little energy left to be in touch with reality. Now, if we want to make a person whole, we have first to understand what is merely fantasy and irrationality, and we have to discover where one is in touch, and with what. And very often if we work, and we empty out this middle zone of fantasy, this *maya,* then there is the experience of *satori,* of waking up. Suddenly the world is *there.* You wake up from a trance like you wake up from a dream. You're all there again."[2]

I ask people to go into their fantasy world and to represent in art form what they find there—to empty out this area and look at its contents. Often that is a first step to achieving a new creative synthesis of two old enemies. Says Perls, "Instead of being divided between *maya* and reality, we can integrate these two, and if *maya* and reality are integrated, we call it art. Great art is real, and great art is at the same time an illusion. Fantasy can be creative, but it's creative only if you have the fantasy, whatever it is, in the *now.*"[3]

Now, having integrated fantasy with the art experience, I can speak of the process of getting more self-support for personal growth. Your personality is made up of many parts; some may seem strange to you; to be truly self-supporting, you need to explore areas that are alien

[2] Fritz S. Perls, *Gestalt Therapy Verbatim* (Moab, Ut.: Real People Press, 1969), p. 50. © Copyright 1969 Real People Press. Reprinted by permission.
[3] *Ibid. p. 50.*

to you. You can have more of you available to yourself when you do this. Laura Perls describes this learning to know all of oneself: "The process could be compared with the creation of a work of art (the highest form of integrated and integrating human experience), in which the conflict between a multitude of incompatible and unmanageable experiences is realized only at the point where the means for its interpretation and transformation become available."[4]

Supported by both Laura Perls and Fritz Perls, I can state that people do fantasize in their own ways; I assume you do, too. I find that some of us can use fantasy as a way of finding reality. Art experience can offer a way for you to try this, and the art form you create can provide you with a means of interpretation and a potential for transformation.

For some people—practical, sensible, no-nonsense folk who pride themselves on always being realistic—the idea of fantasizing is anathema.

A man watches a football game on television, identifying with his team; he cheers and stomps, curses, and feels defeat or triumph. When the game is finished, he says, "Boy! We really showed them a thing or two," or "We'd have made that touchdown if it hadn't been so muddy on the field!" If you hadn't seen him sitting there in his comfortable armchair all those hours, you'd think from his talk that he had actually been out there, battling and giving his all for the team. In his fantasy, he really was fighting to win that game, but don't tell him that he was fantasizing all Saturday afternoon because he is a practical man and doesn't have any patience with things that aren't realistic.

His wife is taking art lessons. She has been painting all that Saturday afternoon. She is excited and says, "I finally found out how to get the colors to express what I wanted them to in this picture. See that spiral red form? That's how I feel inside, now that I'm pregnant!" And he says, "Well, I'm glad you like what you're doing if it makes you happy, but I don't see any sense to it. It's just some paper and paint, and you haven't made a picture of anything real, anyway. If you like playing around with this art, it's okay by me, but don't get carried away. Your getting so excited about your insides seems rather morbid to me."

Joe and Jane are another couple I know. One night, Joe comes home from the office, seems extra sober during dinner, and then says, "I've been thinking. I could retire next year and have enough pension coming in so we could live on it if we were careful. What I'd like to do is buy a few acres out in the country and build just the kind of house we want. I could farm on a small scale and make some honest use of all those tools in the basement to make furniture. I'm tired of just sitting around all day in an air-conditioned office. I want to get outside and make something that I can feel proud of."

[4] Paul D. Pursglove, *Recognitions in Gestalt Therapy,* (New York: Harper & Row, 1971), p. 45.

Jane, always practical, says, "Now, Joe, be reasonable. You keep talking about this idea of building us a house and growing our own food. You're just daydreaming. It's not practical. What we should do is buy into one of those retirement condominiums that they're advertising on television. They include central heat and air conditioning, and they have caretakers and managers and social clubs and cable television, and they take care of everything you want. They even have a hobby shop where you could make some little wood carvings if you want to. But you wouldn't have to do anything. That's the sensible thing for us to do."

One person's reality is another's fantasy. And most people are a bit apologetic about their own fantasizing. Yet we all do it, in one way or another, and those who say they are completely realistic are deluding themselves. They are lying to themselves, or they are completely out of touch with themselves. They are also denying one of their richest resources for living with their fullest reality.

Rollo May says:

Fantasy is one expression of imagination. Imagination is the home of intentionality, and fantasy one of its languages. (I use fantasy here in its original meaning of 'able to represent, to make visible.') Fantasy is the language of the total self, communicating, offering itself, trying on for size. It is the language of "I wish/I will"—the imaginative projection of the self into the situation. And if one cannot do this, he will not be present in any situation, whether his body is there or not. Fantasy assimilates reality, then pushes it to a new depth.[5]

Bless Rollo May for writing in beautiful prose what I know to be true through experience! And bless art media that provide the language with which anyone is "able to represent, to make visible" his fantasies for assimilating his wholeness and for intercommunicating with the reality perceptions of others.

Have you ever lain flat on your back on the cool beach sand and looked up at the moon, fantasizing that you can feel the earth's turning beneath you, holding your body close to its surface while you feel the moon's pull in your blood? Have you felt your kinship with the tides as they respond to the distant orbits of the sun and the moon? Have you watched a seedling turn its new leaf growth always toward the life-giving light? Have you felt among growing things how interdependent your breathing is with theirs? Have you looked into the eyes of a newborn baby and known that he has just accomplished the miraculous

[5] Rollo May, "Love and Will," *Psychology Today*, 1969, **3** (III), 57.

journey from one kind of space into another? An hour ago he floated in liquid darkness; now he thrashes to breathe in a world of gas and light. Have you wakened suddenly from deep sleep, knowing that you have apprehended in your dreaming a vivid integration of insights that your waking self could only vaguely comprehend?

These are some of my reality-fantasies. You name your own, which may be quite different from mine. We can share and enrich each other's capacities for experiencing fully when we are not afraid to reveal our wondrously individual imaginative perceptions. So often we hold back and hide our uniqueness, saying, "If you knew what I was *really* feeling, you'd think I was crazy." So many people are inhibited by the fear that the revelation of their fantasizing would bring onto them the judgment of "crazy," "silly," "stupid," "childish," "morbid," "unrealistic," or "evil." This sort of judgment is handed out by people whose prosaic minds will not recognize their own fantasy life and consequently will surely not accept that of another.

In our culture, we tend to avoid actualizing our individual imaginings in daily living situations; we allow ourselves to experience fantasy only through vicarious participation. We accept the fantasy world of theater, movies, television, poetry, fiction, ritualized ceremonies, and the creation of artists. We even accept the commercialized fantasies used in advertising; although we know that some of the fantastic claims must be lies, we let ourselves believe because we want to.

We want to believe our own fantasies, too, but we are afraid to trust our individual self-imaginings. We are loath to look at them clearly; we suspect some of them may be lies. It is true that some of our fantasies are delusions and some are deceptions that we create and hide behind to avoid seeing what is real. It is equally true that some of our fantasies are our most valid assurances of what is real. How are we to know for ourselves which are delusions and which are truths unless we are willing to open our Pandora's boxes and risk the possible pandemonium that may break loose?

I have known many people who didn't dare go into their own limbo until they were forced to by outside situations and/or inside pressures. However, I have known many daring persons who look on self-exploration as an adventure into innerspace that they choose to make in the interest of their own growth and genuine excitement in living fully—even if some of the fullness includes confusion and pain. Since I think that there comes a time in the life of every person who lives into full adulthood when he must make discriminating choices if he is to grow into maturity—and since I think that choosing wisely for oneself involves using all of one's resources—I advocate self-exploration into the often undiscovered realm of personal fantasy before a crisis in living forces one into crucial decisions.

Naturally, I recommend art media as one way of traveling into your inner world of awareness. Mostly, I have been and will be urging you to experience art media directly by creating your own forms. However, you can, at the same time, find enjoyment, stimulation, and support in projecting yourself into the fantasies portrayed through art media by others. When we can enter the imaginative reality created by someone else, sometimes we not only join that other person in empathetic communication, but we can also welcome a part of ourselves that we have not recognized before.

Through art media we can recognize, too, connections between ourselves and other selves and what is happening in our common environment. Marshall McLuhan says, "Art as radar acts as an 'early alarm system,' as it were, enabling us to discover social and psychic targets in lots of time to prepare to cope with them. This concept of the arts as prophetic contrasts with the popular idea of them as mere self-expression."[6] McLuhan is referring to art as media for cultural communication, like a "state of the nation" message that we can use as radar for becoming aware of future social and technological developments. I agree and add that we can gauge our own personal developments through our alertness in picking up signals from our participation as observers of the art productions of others.

Art is never "mere self-expression"; whether we are making our own forms or watching someone else's creations, we are actively both receiving and giving out messages. Your preferences for certain kinds of media signal messages to you; your choices of what you listen to, what you read, what you watch, what you attend all indicate your personality pattern. You can grow a lot in self-awareness just by watching yourself watching.

All art productions are fantasies made real, and all convey a message. I cannot imagine that there is anyone who is not affected by the many messages he receives daily from art media: billboards, photographs, illustrations, and paintings; music on radio, records, tapes, and in concerts; words in newspapers, magazines, and books; and imagery on television, movies, and the stage. In other words, everyone inevitably receives messages from art media, but some people seem to be quite oblivious that they are being affected and so do not integrate the effects into their individual awareness.

Those who choose art as their medium can transmit their messages in various ways. Says McLuhan, "Art, like games, is a translator of experience. What we have already felt or seen in one situation we are suddenly given in a new kind of material. Games, likewise, shift familiar experience into new forms, giving the bleak and the blear side of things sudden luminosity."[7]

[6] Marshall McLuhan, *Understanding Media: The Extensions of Man,* p. xi. Copyright © 1964 by Marshall McLuhan. This and all other quotes from the same source are used with permission of McGraw-Hill Book Company.
[7] *Ibid.,* p. 214.

Just as we all fantasize, we all play games of one sort or another. I don't mean we assume false roles in order to manipulate someone else, as Eric Berne describes in *Games People Play.* Instead, I mean that, as individuals and as groups, we contrive situations in which we can express and extend ourselves in a different medium from the one we use in routine living. Calling his game-playing a diversion, a man may say he's "getting away from it all" whether he's frisking with a bunny at a Playboy Club or sweating with an iron on a golf course. He's not "getting away from it all," though; he's getting closer to another aspect of himself—his play and games are ways of self-extension. They are ways of fantasizing, too—whether with bunny or golf club, the man is exploring his prowess in game-playing fantasy, and I assume he can bring quite a bit of artistry into either activity.

Playboy Clubs and golf games are not for everybody, but there are plenty of other games; we each choose the kind of game-playing fantasy that is related to our individual life realities in some way. I can even applaud the phony bunny-girl bit of fun if no better fantasy is available, because, quoting McLuhan once again, I agree that "for fun or games to be welcome, they must be an echo of workaday life. On the other hand, a man or society without games is one sunk in the zombie trance of the automaton. Art and games enable us to stand aside from the material pressures of routine and convention, observing and questioning."[8]

Having gone a long way around from Rollo May through Marshall McLuhan, both of whom accept fantasy, art, and games as expressions of reality, I will come back to the home base of gestalt experience by way of the fantasy-realities of science fiction. I have long been addicted to science fiction, using that genre to mirror my own explorations beyond familiar workaday living into another view of possible realities. I prefer fantasy-fiction about people, like what Ray Bradbury writes with fey humor and respectful compassion for all of us. Says Bradbury, "The ability to 'fantasize' is the ability to survive. It's wonderful to speak about this subject because there have been so many wrong-headed people dealing with it. We're going through a terrible period in art, in literature and living, in psychiatry and psychology. The so-called realists are trying to drive us insane, and I refuse to be driven insane."[9]

I am assuming that Bradbury's "so-called realists," McLuhan's "zombie," May's nonfantasizer, and my human making like a robot are of the same breed. And I am also assuming that none of you is inevitably stuck in that mold. I believe that anyone with zest for living fully and

[8] *Ibid.,* p. 210.
[9] M. H. Hall, "A Conversation with Ray Bradbury and Chuck Jones, The Fantasy Makers," *Psychology Today,* 1968, **11** (I), 28–29. This entire issue is devoted to fantasy and reality.

courage for exploring his fantasies realistically can find many ways open to him. Experiencing and communicating through art is one access medium. Few of you will produce films for mass media, books, television shows, or have your art forms shown to millions, but each of you can, if you choose, produce your own one-man shows. You can invite your friends, colleagues, families, and even some non-friends to see your fantasies-made-real; you may affect other observers and free communication between you to go to deeper levels. Most immediately, you can each become a more sensitive and discerning viewer and audience for your own life drama; with a little bit of faith in your individual capacities, you can even create some fantastic effects in your personal life process.

PEOPLE IN PROCESS

I stubbornly refuse to use the term *case history* when I present my observation of the ongoing process shown in the life of another person. I can't resist quoting one of the many definitions Mr. Webster includes for "case": "A divided tray for types"! Although that definition refers to printing paraphernalia, I sometimes think it is also applicable to those reports in which people are "typed" and thus put into one section of a vast case-history tray. History, according to my handy desk dictionary, is "a narration of facts and events arranged chronologically with their causes and effects." That definition is a bit dated in our age of relativity, field theories, and undeclared real wars even when it is used to present world happenings; and it certainly is not appropriate for one human to attempt to reduce the life drama of another into a manila-folder-sized case history. I sympathize with those who must, for expediency's sake, write and file those factual documents. They have to do so; I don't and won't.

To me, a *fact* is one of those very few things that I know for sure and that have some relevance to the much larger picture of my personal reality. What are the facts of my exhilaration when sudden rain breaks the smothering heat of a summer afternoon? You can measure the drop in air temperature in degrees; you can measure the amount of rainfall in inches. Those are facts, but what do they have to do with how I feel when I breathe the cool smells of quickly dampened earth and feel my salty sweat washed away by pelting drops of fresh rain?

What are the facts about a clay figure that your hands form with rhythmic caressing movements? You use 20 pounds of quarry tile red clay, with such-and-such a density at such-and-such a temperature. Facts, yes. But so what? What has fact to contribute to your sense of some sublime image that you have created from an inert hunk of dirt and water?

Art that is aesthetically satisfying cannot be described in terms of measurable facts. Neither can the form made by the neophyte who never knew before that he could create something expressive out of materials that do nothing but respond to the energy of the maker's hands. You produce a form that is your form. You say, "This is my form. This is how I feel." You don't have to be more explicit than that. That's real, and no facts explaining why are needed or wanted.

I am in a dilemma about writing this part of my book. I tell you that I've used art as experience and expression for half a century, that I've taught others my way of doing so over 20 years, and that for the last five years I've led hundreds of groups in therapeutic art experiences. I say to myself, "Surely out of all of these years of participation and observation, I must have some factual material to pass on to you who read this." My little red notebooks are crammed with what I've written through these years, but when I read my notes I find descriptions and questions, not facts. I find some observations, though, that may be valid if we recognize that my perception is selective. Like anyone else, I tend to perceive what I want to; I can't be totally objective even when I try to be—which isn't very often.

I won't even try to write objective facts; I will write brief descriptions of some people as I know them through their art experiences. Our relationships have been and still are more than casual; in groups and on a one-to-one basis we have shared weal and woe; we have known each other well and long. But we do not know everything about each other, nor have we always been together, nor will we be forever.

Helen

Helen is a black woman—intelligent, dynamic. At 35 she has succeeded in her career as a community development worker, moving through her professional and social life with both blacks and whites in such a confident manner that people respond to her with respectful admiration. She is strikingly handsome, dresses colorfully, makes friends easily, and fights vigorously with people who violate her moral code. When I met her five years ago I saw her as regal, queenly, and dominant. She seemed so sure of herself that I was intimidated. The first evening we spent together she made it quite plain that she had no interest in joining groups unless they were working on some project that might bring tangible results toward helping her people. Proud of her own realism, she was impatient with "therapy groups where white middle-class adults spend hours talking about their emotional woes when so many poor people are dealing with the immediate reality of getting jobs and money for survival." I couldn't and wouldn't argue with her. Obviously the work she was and is doing deserves the time and energy Helen and others give to it.

However, in the last five years, Helen and I have found that our two ways of working with people are not mutually exclusive. She has participated in groups not directly aimed at social action: she has made many of us more aware of our failure to deal with the position of blacks; she, herself, has become more aware of her personal emotional needs, which have little to do with black-white problems. Participation in art experience groups has been a major factor in Helen's finding out for herself and being able to reveal to a few of us some of her inner turmoil, unsureness, shyness, and unadmitted longing for intimate contact with her peers in a non-professional context.

Her first experience in painting was not in a group. Out of curiosity she went with me to the "Art Barn," an old building in the country that was about to fall down and that I was using as a studio for groups doing art work. Helen laughed at my suggestion that she do a painting just for the fun of it. She had never painted; the idea of her being an artist seemed absurd to her, but she couldn't resist the challenge of the jars of color. So she painted enthusiastically, being very voluble, all the while deriding herself: "I don't know how to paint. This is silly. I don't even know how to mix colors to get brown!" At the same time she *was* painting with bold forthright strokes; while she was saying with words that she didn't know how, she was acting as if she knew exactly what she wanted to portray and wasn't going to waste any time in getting that painting done.

Figure 5. Helen, "Autumn Tree."

That first painting represented several facets of Helen's personality (see Figure 5, "Autumn Tree"). The strong, centrally dominant tree form moves upward with assurance; it is a no-nonsense tree trunk made with quick strong brush marks. Helen communicated authoritatively that "I am me." The vibrantly orange and yellow background has two other squared-off, growing tree forms. When she had filled in the page with warm colors, Helen was dissatisfied. She wanted some lightness of movement, "Some leaves or something lively; how can I paint in leaves moving?" With my usual refusal to tell anybody how to express himself, I answered something like, "It's your painting. Do it anyway you want to." She swirled in the gray lines of movement and squiggled on some amorphous black, and there was her liveliness. She was satisfied, saying that the painting expressed the way she felt—warm, excited, growing, feeling relaxed in the country, away from the pressures under which she worked in the city.

Some time after that impromptu session, Helen joined the art experience group that Miles Vich and I led in San Francisco. Twelve of us met weekly for a three-hour session in the top floor of an old Victorian house in the ghetto area of San Francisco.

These groups were experimental, unstructured, and oriented toward personal growth; the participants were adults who were responsible, functioned well in their private lives, could be counted on to provide their own emotional support, if necessary, and could comprehend what was and was not appropriate in the group. We all felt free to risk being open and direct with each other. Miles and I participated in the group as actively as anyone else.

The sessions were informal; these were non-group, self-directed people, and there was no pressure for togetherness. Nevertheless, the members spontaneously rallied around anyone who seemed to be in trouble or who was taking up too much space—literally or figuratively—in that small, intimate studio.

At the beginning of each session, we usually gathered for a brief time to talk so that anyone who wanted to could bring out words, thoughts, and feelings about himself and others. Sometimes these talks led to people working together, but mostly each person did his own sort of art work with whatever materials he chose.

For two years those groups were a source of both inspiration and exasperation for quite a few of us. We learned a lot about freedom, autonomy, intimacy, and responsibility—and most of this we expressed with art materials.

In this group and in others that followed, Helen explored with art materials the felt-needs, emotional blocks, and thinking patterns of which she was unaware. She is still competent, autonomous, and fiercely independent in her life and work, but she is also much more open to experience, more trusting of others, and more willing to admit her vulnerability, knowing that at least some of her problems and solutions have no basis in her skin color. She and I have become friends and exchange confidences as well as recipes.

During the first few sessions, Helen surprised herself and others in the group with her ability to paint as if she had had years of training. Her sense of design was excellent, her compositions were sure and strong, and her use of color discriminatingly forceful. For some time she enjoyed her newly discovered capacity for creating paintings that pleased her and did not interest herself in any other kind of group participation. Having fun exploring a new competency was enough for then.

However, in that group of strong personalities, she could not resist becoming involved with others as individualized as herself. Her first overt emotional contact occurred when she painted in one large area with Miles. I watched the two of them struggle wordlessly for domination of the common territory of their shared sheet of paper; using paint-loaded brushes as weapons, they fought for the triumph of obliterating each other's gains in terms of space and color. Helen used black and Miles red: she was on the defensive, not pushing to invade his area of painting until he deliberately covered all of her black areas except around the edges. Then Helen, forced to paint in only a corner, took the offensive and spread thick black all over the board. Expressing fierce determination, she would not let herself be pushed around even symbolically. Her attitude of amused detachment gave way to active hostility; her clenched jaws, hard breathing, and slashing strokes were not those of a cool, organized worker. She was fighting for what was hers!

The painting wasn't much to look at aesthetically, but Helen's lively face was. She was panting and speechless, and she was triumphant. She had openly expressed her fury with a man, had not been annihilated, and was applauded by others for revealing her feelings instead of hiding behind her mask of indifference to masculine aggression. After the furor of the battle, Helen went off to a corner of the studio, very quiet and pensive. Talking to no one for the rest of the evening, she covered a small sheet of paper with wide smooth horizontal bands of blue, soft and serene. I saw her gentleness and tenderness, then, for the first time; I saw her quiescent sadness, too, but I said nothing. Her furious contest with Miles had exhausted her. She needed to withdraw into solitude.

The next week Helen chose to paint alone. Again she chose to work away from the group instead of joining in the sporadic verbal exchanges people made when they were excited by what they were doing or by some interaction with each other. Helen was completely absorbed in what she was doing. Her intensity and tension were evident; though she said nothing, she huddled over her painting protectively. When she had finished she turned it face down on the floor and moved away from it; she seemed shocked, bewildered, confused. Though Helen acted as if she had disowned the painting and did not want attention focused on it, I trusted my intuition that she did want to share it with us though she was too inhibited to ask for what she wanted. At my suggestion she showed the painting to the group, saying that she wasn't sure what it represented to her.

The imagery in "Monster Man" (see Plate 1) is strikingly direct and powerfully communicative. The group was sobered by the impact of Helen's revelation; we all realized the importance of this to her. She seemed almost stunned by her own message, as if she had discovered a different dimension in which she was disoriented and unable to comprehend how to deal with this awareness. The members of the group did not analyze, criticize, or advise; we conveyed our understanding and respected Helen's wish to keep private for a while.

Helen answered only in monosyllables; obviously deeply moved, she was still unable to express her emotions directly. No one pushed her. Later she and I talked privately about the painting and what it meant to her. Recently I asked her if she'd like to write for publication in this book whatever she wanted to say about that painting and any others that were significant to her. She agreed with anxious excitement and wrote the following without reading anything I had written about her:

Painting the monster man was not planned or anticipated; instead, his form just exuded from somewhere deep down inside of me. I started painting by covering a plain sheet of white paper with purple in the same manner that I often started working in the art group. Purple held such an indescribable fascination for me. I loved the color, and it stirred inside me all the passion I was capable of feeling at the time.

The color red affected me in just the opposite way. I could not bear red; it just turned me off with its ugliness, representing blood, injury, and raw meat. So I attempted to overcome my hatred of red and my inability to use it any place in my life by mixing it with purple. After working for some time with the two colors and subduing the red with purple and creating a texture on the paper that I liked, I found myself feeling completely compelled to try to paint on this background a man as I conceived a man to be. Man, to be feared for his strengths and weaknesses, whose corrupted intelligence is frequently used to connive cruel and selfish acts against others, particularly women. Man, capable of admirable physical strength in his body, but who over-rates the strength and importance of his penis.

While painting, I was fully engrossed in creating this creature and lost all awareness of the six to eight other people in the room. This hulking form came forth from me with such single-minded intensity that I lost consciousness of the presence of other people in the room. I know now that if I had not been able to forget the group's presence, this painting would never have happened.

Finally, after about one and one-half hours of struggling with my feelings and trying to convey them with the paints, I realized that a group of people was present and that at least some of them probably had been observing me expressing some extremely personal feelings I had never expressed verbally. Feeling trapped, cornered, and completely exposed, I did not want to turn around to face the group. I was quite tempted to snatch the picture from the wall, ball it up, and throw it into the wastebasket but realized that this would only attract more attention and further expose me.

Surreptitiously I removed the painting from the wall and contemplated my turning around to face the group of people, which I now knew was present. I visualized the eyes of everyone in the room on me and dreaded that moment of turning around. I felt completely naked both physically and mentally and kept my back to the group as long as possible and probably would have remained that way indefinitely except that I wanted to remove the picture from the wall and dispose of it as quietly and quickly as possible. I had to face the group in order to save myself. I turned around, and no one appeared to be noticing me. I quickly shoved the picture under a table and glanced around the room. One of the co-leaders of the group peered under the table at the picture, and I sank inside because I knew that my innermost feelings and thoughts had been exposed and observed by someone with an acute eye for knowing what is going on inside others. Another member of the group came over and hugged me, and I sank even deeper knowing that I had exposed myself even further, and I wanted to disappear completely or cry, but I couldn't do either.

The whole image of myself as a strong, unemotional, unfeeling, self-sufficient, unexposed person disappeared, and I admitted for the first time in my life that I was a human being; I admitted for the first time in my life that I could hurt, and I admitted for the first time in my life that I had weaknesses.

Since that time, three years ago, Helen has been involved not only in her career, but also in an experimental search for her identity as a woman. Her seeking is sporadic and cautious. She still holds to her mores of dignity, integrity, and decency and acts accordingly. Her experiments in intimate relationships with men or women and with groups are structured so that she does not needlessly violate the cultural values that she has accepted. She still pulls away from any situation in which she feels pushed or coerced into more closeness than she is ready for. She still shows hostility toward men, and this gets in her way both professionally and personally.

The change I see in Helen is her recognition of her vulnerability and especially her acceptance of it, her need for support from others, and, most important, her willingness to let herself be known as she is, without having to hide her needs.

One of Helen's greatest needs was to let go of her lifelong pattern of single-minded planning and directing of her energies toward achievement of difficult goals. To accomplish these goals she had had to be in control of herself and the situation; she had struggled to earn each success, and she had developed her capacities for competition, toughness, independence, and perseverance. She had learned how to work hard, but she had not learned how to play. The use of art materials gave her an opportunity to play, to let things happen instead of making them happen. In her paintings she was not goal-oriented or competitive; she was exploring a medium that was new to her, a process rather than a plan, an experience rather than an achievement. She enjoyed the process and the experience. Relaxing her usual purposefulness, she dropped her defenses and expressed more freely what she was feeling. Having already revealed her emotional states in the paintings made it possible to talk about her inner life with others in the group. Being understood and accepted sympathetically by the group has given Helen experiences in trusting others; this trust helps her now in feeling and being freer to accept close friendships, to experience man-woman relationships with much less fear, and to make decisions based on her real desires instead of her old compulsive behavior of having to *win* no matter what the cost to her. She can laugh, be sad, excited, discouraged, enthusiastic, and she can let others share her problems without cutting us off by hiding her eyes and her humanness from us.

The last painting Helen did in the art group, "Moods" (Plate 1), obviously made her feel good, but she didn't talk to us about it. She had it framed and hung it in her office above her desk. When I asked her what it meant to her, she said that through this painting experience she had become aware of what black meant to her, personally. She wanted to write her realizations in her own words:

Black means a deep, dark, unknown place and fear of
that place. Black means a tremendous and awesome
power. Black is the color of being in a roomful of people

and feeling apart from them and not being able to respond to their love, openness, or needs. Black is being hemmed into a corner and an inability to overcome or even understand that which hems me into the corner. Black is the color I wear to funerals, and it is the color I associate with maturity and sophistication—I could not wait until I was old enough to wear a black dress. I am black, and sometimes I am beautiful, but at other times I am black, obnoxious, scared, and ugly. Black is the color of the enemy until he proves himself otherwise.

I could not have chosen any color other than black to paint the "man-monster."

The painting "Moods" began from the deep, dark, frightened place where I was when the group gathered, and I realized I was in a roomful of people, many of whom I knew personally and liked. Yet I felt thousands of miles away from them and wanted to remain that way. Hemmed in by my feelings of anxiety and needing an escape route, I began painting on a sheet of paper with black color because that was the color that best described my feelings. As the painting progressed, I felt a release from the "hemmed in the corner" place where I was when I began. Painting in black and giving in to my feelings seemed to have a very liberating effect on my black mood. I don't know how long I worked with the black color, but I remember that when I began I had the intention of painting the whole sheet of paper black, black, black. In a sense, I painted my way out of the corner and as my mood brightened, my colors brightened. Later, I felt as free and serene as the sky and ocean on a peaceful day and chose colors that conveyed peace and serenity to me. I have always had drastic mood changes but usually attempted to hide them or cover them up. While painting this picture, I made no such attempt but simply painted as I felt.

Finally, I felt bright gaiety that I needed to have stand out from the black, the green, and the blue. Since yellow or gold represents to me a bright new freedom, the breaking of rigidified life patterns, I superimposed the color yellow in a freely moving, gay pattern to represent the feelings I was experiencing near the end of the two-hour group meeting. "Moods" was painted over three years ago, and now it occurs to me that it may represent more than any other painting I have ever done in my past, present, and future. The future at that time would be the present now.

Norman

Norman is not a young man. He has labored as a carpenter-craftsman; he has been teacher and artist. He's been through some rough times, as his painting "Tough Old Tree" (Plate 2) testifies. It was done four years ago in a gestalt workshop during which I led some art experience sessions. Norman spoke of the painting's showing that though he was rough and dark, twisted by time, there was some bright color in the sky behind him and some new growth coming out of his weathered trunk.

Last year, during a training group for art therapists, Norman created the collage, "Accusing Eye" (Plate 2). With wry humor, he laughed at himself that he, so adult in many ways, had not yet grown out of a stripling's feeling of guilt about his natural sexual curiosity; he confided to those of us in the group that every time he looked at a *Playboy* magazine he felt "somebody's eye" looking back at him, saying "Naughty! Naughty!" When we smiled with him and admitted that most of us had at least remnants of this shamed feeling when we responded to slick, full-color nude photos, he said he didn't feel as "tied up" as the man in the tiny photo in the collage. The dark, flower-like form in the lower right expresses the same idea as in "Tough Old Tree": "I am not young and fresh, but I'm alive and growing."

Norman is a perceptive and successful full-time art therapist, guiding patients in art experiences in two clinics.

Cyndy

Cyndy is a psychiatric social worker and an excellent therapist. That's her professional title and capability. More important to me, she is a very human and lovable young woman, living with lusty enthusiasm, with pondering sadness, with cheerful courage. She has participated in art experience groups led by me; I have participated in therapy groups led by her.

We co-lead groups with the central theme of "Being a Woman," using gestalt and art experiences to help us get more in touch with our essential womanhood.

Three years ago, Cyndy drew "I Want" (Plate 2). She did "Perhaps Tomorrow" (Plate 3) recently and wrote her poetic interpretation of both of them.

To me, Cyndy's drawings and words speak of the universal process of longing, growing, stretching, and reaching for a full sense of one's unique identity.

"I Want" (Plate 2)

I want
I try
I try
I squeeze
My opening is not open. I am
Closed.
I burn, trying. Trying to squeeze
Open.
I want tomorrow now.
I cannot happen tomorrow
I happen now.
Only.

"Perhaps Tomorrow" (Plate 3)

Solid
Strong
Wistful, floating
Yellow/white center, I feel
Discomfort, a twist in me, I stop
I cover it with left-over color
Faded color
A part of me I don't know there
I'm not sure I want to
Tho I sense something exciting
Upsetting, delightful, scary,
Ecstatic evil there
Hidden in that white/yellow space.

I want to stay away right now.
Perhaps tomorrow.

Celia

Celia is one of those improbable people who seems to have an inexhaustible capacity for contrasts: she is superbly arrogant and beautifully humble; she is a whirlwind of activity and a quiet pool of contemplation; she is lovingly supportive of others and witheringly astute in refusing to condone weakness; she lives with zestful vitality and with a full awareness of the ever-present inevitability of death.

Celia is a wondrously creative human being. During the last few years, I have known her as a participant in my art experience groups, as a trainee for her profession as art therapist, and as my colleague and friend.

I have known her at times when she was spiraled inward in introspection and at other times when she was sparkling radiantly outward into the world.

Celia's drawings ("Inside Myself," Plate 3; "All Over the Place," Plate 4) were done in art experience groups during several months when Celia was particularly volatile and mercurial; she perceived that she was growing into her own realization that she could be all over the place and yet not lose her beingness inside herself.

Celia describes her drawings:

"Inside Myself" (Plate 3)

My innermost self is the orange center. Surrounding it, the radiating blue lines are my conscious out-reachings into the world. The purple is my subconscious envelope. Those things I am most involved with are closest. The outer rings of unknown experience are as yet blank. The black area is death.

"All Over the Place" (Plate 4)

The whole page is my environment. I am intermixed over, under, and through it as the blue color. The environment is all that I experience and think about—past, present, and future. At some points my color changes its color or form; at others, the reverse is true. Actually, the mutual effects are always happening, always changing. The black is evil, suffering, and so on; the warm colors are the exciting, positive aspects of life. The growing edge of creativity is in the green splashes.

Coeleen

Coeleen did two paintings in the same day during a time when she was facing, forcing, and fearing crucial changes in her way of life. (See Plate 4, "Little Black Boy" and "Stretched Out on the Beach.") As a wife and the mother of four children, she had fantasized that she was looking at life through a telescope that narrowed her vision and brought distant horizons closer to her but at the same time interfered with directly contacting what she saw. Now divorced and seeking a new orientation for her life, she was in a sea of confusion, trying to find a place for her personal, dark, primitive, playful little-boy self while fulfilling her felt maternal desires to remain strong, wise, and supportive for her children.

She spent a full month painting in my studio, and we spent hours daily talking of her feelings, thoughts, and perceptions of what choices were available to her.

In spite of her confusion, or maybe because she did work so hard in recognizing and resolving her conflicts, Coeleen has found that she surely does have what it takes to choose and pursue her own way, being artist, teacher, mother, and woman. She is struggling still, but with confidence that she can and will go further in her courageous determination to keep her feet on the ground at home and also to submerge herself to exciting depths of self-exploration.

Here are some comments Coeleen made after we worked with the paintings.

"Little Black Boy" (Plate 4)

I looked back into the sea, and there in the swirl of the depths was the golden, bejeweled telescope and the Little Black Boy I had left behind.

It felt good to be rid of them. The once beautiful and idealistic telescope I had used to keep me flying and to give me perspective now seemed gaudy and very narrow in vision. It had protected me from dealing with getting my feet on the ground and from seeing the reality of the immediate.

And the Little Boy—knowing but not feeling, sensing but not knowing. A whole lot to be met about the Little Boy. Take me down into the deep, show me around the deep. If we encounter sharks, you distract them from me. Little Boy, free, related with nature, independent, brown and full of sun, having fun, curious, able to risk. Companion. Plays with me. Asks little of me.

Would be sad to give him up. But he's like the Sirens. Could lead me astray.

The Little Black Boy—charming and a pleasant companion—had become a nuisance and diversion from the task at hand.

The threat of being led astray had become very real. If I am led astray, I become a waif—no home, no family, no ties, no base, taking what I can get, living off the land from day to day, getting love where I can find it.

The boy is a pleasant diversion but not what I want. If I internalize the Little Boy, I like what happens to me— more related with nature, more fun, more physical activity, more alive, and curiously creative.

The Little Boy keeps me from being alone.

As I look at the picture now, I see that the Little Boy
appears to be a man getting up, and I fear relating with
this part of me—the dark male adult. The dark man.

"Stretched Out on the Beach" (Plate 4)

The warmth of the sun on my body. Utter total exhaustion. Laid out. Relaxed without the Little Boy or telescope.

Then I look carefully at the painting and consider how
vulnerable I seem. What if the dark man comes out of the
sea? How might he take advantage of me? Rape? Seduc-
tion? Force me into becoming a woman who could face
life as an adult?

And I wonder if I am safe without the comfortable defenses of the telescope and Little Black Boy.

In complete confusion and frustration I am shocked to
see another form in the painting. Instead of totally relaxed,
I seem—I am—a seething monster pounding the beach
with my fists. Kicking and glaring in great anger and pain.

It seems I have worked very hard and am only more
confused. I even wondered if I was able, had what it takes
to pursue further.

Sharon

Sharon is living on many levels all at once; I marvel that she
can move about in the everyday world practically and effectively while
carrying on such a lot of symbolic activity in her inner life. Tiny and
delicate physically, she is inclined to be quiet and still. Only her shining, expressive eyes move about quickly, and she tilts her head from
side to side as if she wants to see things from many angles. When she
feels shy and fearful, Sharon's whole bearing becomes that of a little
girl, on the verge of but never quite giving up her held-back tears. When
she has that look I see the child who learned to go into her closet and
be alone rather than ask for any sort of open emotional expression with
her parents. Her mother says that Sharon was an obnoxious child whom
she has never understood; her father, a quiet, bookish man, dra-
matically taught Sharon that the best thing to do with bad feelings was
to bury them underground; in a planned ceremony the two went out
one evening, dug a hole in the ground, and 6-year-old Sharon was told
to bury her temper and never let it show again.

Sharon learned her lesson well; her conscious suppression
gradually became habitual and her outward behavior fit into the family's
pattern of keeping out of sight anything that might be disturbing. In her

aloneness, Sharon created a fantasy-companion, as many children do, but Sharon's companion was a machine, about which she writes:

> When I was a child I had a machine, smooth, well-honed, slick, and a constant source of a noise in my head. The sound was like grease running through several cylinders of very smooth steel. The noise was high-pitched and re-lentless. It was a vivid experience for many years. I remem-ber being alone. I felt the aloneness, and the machine would take up all the space in my head, drowning out the everyday sounds, the everyday feelings, providing a transi-tion into unreality as the house got quieter and quieter. The feeling of sliding through all those unending cylinders, be-ing flattened and changing form from bone to liquid, from empty quiet to a roaring silence, from being me to being a substance rolling through a vast process. I would lie on a bed in a room and not recognize my surroundings. A heavi-ness and flatness would seem to overcome me and every-thing looked unreal and strange. I would try to break the feeling by getting up and going out of the house. I would see the outside and the trees and I would concentrate on looking at them until I would reach some kind of balance. I would watch the sky and pretend there was a noise com-ing from the space until I could hear that sound instead of the roaring in my head. As the sky sound would increase I would recognize familiar things, the house and me and where I was sitting and it would all be over.

Sharon went to college, painted, went to a New York art school on a scholarship, and worked for the New York State Council of the Arts. Her inventive techniques for three-dimensional print-making brought her success but not much happiness. She tried psychotherapy; that didn't seem to help. Her prints were in galleries, and she was in limbo. She took LSD and was shocked out of lethargy; on the drug she felt transported beyond all individuality and felt ecstasy in belonging with all-beingness. She saw joys in non-ego-involvement and envisioned wondrous release in non-being. But she was frightened, too; when she saw herself in a mirror, Sharon saw only translucency. Was that what she wanted—to lose her identity in cosmic unity before she'd ever lived here on this earth? Sharon didn't know. She and a new husband, who was little more than another body in lostness, began wandering. John drove the car; Sharon sat and passively watched the world go by. "It" was "out there, fascinating" but none of "it" was here.

Back in San Francisco, Sharon functioned on a sort of mini-mal level, limiting herself to superficial involvements. But when her father developed terminal cancer, she chose to be with him during the long months of his dying. At his request, Sharon and her father together did what they could to help him express his buried feelings; he grieved that he had repressed so much of himself and hoped that Sharon would live more freely. After her father died, though, she felt more deadened than ever and could not involve herself deeply in art or anything else. Sharon realized how much she had cut off her creativity when she saw in a stranger's home a three-dimensional print that she'd made two years before and now could not recognize or remember as her own creation. Shortly afterwards she began coming to art therapy groups and then to weekly private sessions with me. For the first year, Sharon resisted expressing herself with art forms; given a large sheet of paper, she would draw tiny, delicate decorations in one corner and was in-articulate about them. Six months ago Sharon told me that she was "making little things" at home; she "enjoyed tinkering," she said. She made gifts for people, grew potted plants, decorated her apartment for Christmas—small things, but all of her own creation. She brought small, neat, black and white collages to our sessions, discussing how she was beginning to discover elements in them that related to her individuality. A month ago she brought the four forms shown in Figures 6, 7, 8, and 9.

Figure 6. Sharon, "Aspect I."

About six inches high, made from plastic, glass, cotton, and metal, they are very personally Sharon's. At my suggestion, she began expressing her thoughts and feelings by writing. At first this was difficult for her, but now she pours out words, pages and pages of them. In her own way, she describes her self-trait figures:

"Aspect I"

I am obscure, unclear, non-functional, split, non-directional. I am soft and dream-like, with sharp tangents of reality and discomfort. I neither radiate nor direct. I feel helpless and static. My movement is dependent—I can be picked up, placed, and given meaning by an "other." I can also be ignored, passed over, unseen. I can be loved or unloved, unhappy or happy, observant but indecisive, a willing object. I am between a dream and a reality. Life becomes an echo.

"Aspect II"

I am definite, definitive, directed. My movement starts slowly with a spiraling to conclusions. I am unreasonable, brilliant, angry, rash, permanent, stubborn, and purposeful. I am right, tall, and impenetrable. I have no feeling, but I have logical progressions of a third sense. I reach an end, lose connections with the spiral or process or why, and I become implacable, dreamless, determined, and compassionless. I am not here to be loved or loving. I am here to do and to be. There is no echo, I am the voice and the conception. Brittle and breakable.

"Aspect III"

I am in balance, shorter but functioning. I can both feel and be at the same time. I combine softness with balance and brittle receptivity. I am open to change that I can maintain in various positions. I can be delighted and graceful, useful and willing. I have a synthesis of dream and reality. I am non-linear; I can be absurd but not dismissed. I do not alarm, nor do I feel alarmed or vulnerable to breakage. I am perhaps content with the image I am.

Figure 7. Sharon, "Aspect II."

Figure 8. Sharon, "Aspect III."

Figure 9. Sharon, "Aspect IV."

"Aspect IV"

I must combine my dream-observer with real-life situations. Softness can combine with sharpness and still give a pleasing feeling. I can joke about my situation because I am self-willed and not an object of a stranger's needs. I can work with my own needs and experiment with combinations of feelings. I can destroy myself when I feel I need to destroy an unworkable aspect of me. If I do it, it's okay; I need the time to reach my own conclusions. I can laugh and give my experience to others 'cause I did it myself.

Sharon is now exploring her own experiences through art, with her own intelligence and imagination; recently she wrote: "I don't use my machine any longer, but I have developed a real feel for edges. I can sense an edge, or a limit, or a closing off of space and time and sound when I am in an uncomfortable situation. . . . I am trying to learn the process of expanding this space without the fear of edges, without the tendency to get lost in another, and without the need to scrap the whole picture if I can't find my place."

Sharon is finding her place: she is working for a public service agency part time and is also acquiring a clientele for her free-lance services as a designer. She feels that she will have an agency in a few years and is excited about her possibilities. More important, Sharon is increasingly self-determining; she is realistically expanding to fit recognized spaces in her own potential.

These brief vignettes are unenclosed, open-ended images of the here-and-now awareness of some people in process. More eloquent than any words I can say are their own self-perceptions, both graphic and verbal.

Their stories neither begin nor end. As someone said:

Perhaps all stories should begin with the word "and." Perhaps they should end with the word "and," too. It would remind us that no experience ever begins: there was always something that preceded it. What really began, for us, was our awareness of something going on. At the end, the word "and" would remind us that no story ever really ends—something more will happen after. Thus, it may be said that we live in the world of *et cetera*. There is always more to start with than we can take into account. There is always more to say than we can possibly say. There is always more to end with than we can imagine.[10]

[10] "Communications," *Kaiser Aluminum News*, n.d. **3** (XXIII), 2.

Part Two

ART EXPERIENCE
FOR CONTACT AND
COMMUNICATION

Chapter Four

BEING *AWARE* AND GIVING ATTENTION

ALL IN PROCESS

We live in a cosmos of processes; we don't agree about what, when, and how or even if there are first causes, final ends, eternal expandings and contractings, or endless creations and destructions. Scientists discuss the process of our universe: there's the big-bang theory of how our solar system started and there's the steady state theory, which sounds less violent. I listen, fascinated, and don't argue; I can't comprehend such vast goings-on and there's nothing I can do about them, anyway. I am told, too, that on this planet, even our terra firma masses don't stay put. They've been wandering the globe for millions of years, restlessly pushing each other around, thrusting mountain ranges upward, sinking flat lands under brine, spewing molten rock from the icy seas to form new surfaces in Iceland, threatening to grind our West coast into the Pacific. This process comes a bit closer to home; I've tromped the rough volcanic terrain of Iceland; I've experienced minor earthquakes right here. Still, I can't interact with these natural processes; they take their own course irrespective of my influence.

With people, though, I can meet on a down-to-earth basis and we can affect each other as we change in our living situations. We can be aware that we are all in process; also, we can, individually and collectively, influence our own processes to lesser and greater extents.

One way to increase the autonomy of our own life-style is to become more actively aware of what is going on in our living. Something is happening to us all the time; some of the time we don't have to accept passively this being-happened-to, like lava being forced to boil upward and then flow downward, destroying mindlessly. We have conscious minds; we paid dearly for them when we ate that apple and got ourselves exiled from innocence. Now that we are conscious that we are conscious, we'd best use that facility for taking part in shaping the kinds of further evolving we're into.

Before we impose radical changes on our living patterns, though, it would be wise to discover what already exists in our lifestyles. What's the stuff we have to build with? How's the actual reality of what we are now likely to fit into that elaborate scheme of what we should be when? Let's take time to get in touch with ourselves as we are and find out what materials we have available before we design and plan to move into new personality structures. To do this consciously, we must first pay attention to our present *modus operandi;* we must make contact with more of our being than appears habitually; we must become more aware of our total configurations, our total gestalt.

All of the people in process are using art media as one way of exploring their present living gestalts. Through discovering how they are now, they can focus their attention on those personal traits that are the building blocks in their individualized life structures. They are looking at the whole picture of themselves, with their minds open for recognizing resources and strengths as well as problems and weaknesses.

FUNCTIONING FULLY

The people I described in Chapter Three are all working in the broad field of "people-helping." They are professionally responsible not only for recognizing their individual needs but also for paying attention to and offering aid in solving others' problems. To some of their clients and patients, these people seem super-human; sometimes they must act almost as if they were! For the sake of those less adequate than themselves, they must sometimes cover their fears, hold back their tears, stifle their anger, and restrain negative feelings. For balanced expressiveness they participate in the art experience, where they give and take permission to act out with materials and words the most neglected parts of themselves. Often these repressed and sometimes suppressed emotional states seem crazy to those who define sanity in terms that exclude intense and apparently irrational feelings and thoughts. It would be quite possible for someone of a quick judgmental bent to look at the art and word forms of these people in process and pronounce them insane or at least given to psychotic episodes. My own evaluation of the episodes presented here is that their open enactment in an accepting and supportive environment is a positive necessity for the sensitive, perceptive people who spend so much of their time trying to be super-sane in our perplexing culture.

I find special joy and fulfillment in helping to provide media and milieu for responsible professional people to use to get in touch with their own craziness as well as their creativity. In our society we must be aware of and attend to those who are damaged, crippled, retarded, inarticulate, and inadequate in coping with ordinary problems; we must continue to do what we can to help them function well. But we err when we neglect those who are able to cope with extraordinary problems—both professionals in people-helping and those who help people in a personal capacity. These above-average people can and do help others, but often the price is frighteningly high, and all of us pick up part of the bill when we overload our fully functioning people. If we do not allow leeway for our highly bred work horses to kick up their heels some of the time, they may—and often do—kick off their traces entirely and find new pastures to gambol in. I feel that we must be aware of and give attention to the real needs of people-helpers for time and freedom to explore their own dark/light inner experience. Without outlets for expressing their natural and normal idiosyncratic feelings and thoughts, their pent-up emotions all too often precipitate emotional explosions that truly obliterate reality for them.

The people in process I write about are sensitive and perceptive; they recognize their need for expression in the here and now. They are not avoiding their own humanity; they are letting off emotional steam for their sanity's sake; they regress and express not only in the service of their own egos, but also in the interest of being able to function more fully in the service of others.

For instance, looking at Norman's collage, "Accusing Eye" (Plate 2), we see that it is dominated by a nude female torso; the figure has no head, no arms, no legs, no genitals, and moreover, Norman has cut out a section of one breast and replaced it with a large, staring eye. The sadistic work of a sex-ridden maniac? Far from it! This collage represents Norman's sane and honest determination to deal openly with his sexual fantasies instead of hiding them behind a facade of "I'm too mature to harbor such crazy fancies!" He made the collage in a professional group training program. We had met weekly for a year; we encouraged each other to express our absurdities and irrationalities as well as our dignities and reasonablenesses. We even allowed each other a bit of self-pity.

At the time of this expression of Norman's, he and his wife had agreed on a trial separation; living alone and celibate, naturally he thought about sex. Being in his mid-fifties and not a Casanova, he didn't go around seducing available women. He thought about it, though; in fact, he brooded, pondered, wondered, and in his loneliness got himself all tied up in guilt and shame. He was loath to talk about it with his more sedate colleagues and fearful that some of his frustration would spill over into his interactions with patients. One evening when our group was involved in the project of portraying "what is the figure in the background of my life right now," Norman made and sheepishly presented the collage to the rest of us.

The background, he said, represented the values he'd been taught by a strong-minded mother, the formally designed contrasting pattern of mostly red and black indicating stylized, inflexible codes of right and wrong. Especially in attitudes toward women, Norman's background allowed no deviations from socially acceptable mores. These restrictions kept him tied tightly into limited experiences shown in the small, bound figure of a man in the bottom center. To the left of the tiny man is an upward-growing dark flower, unfolding toward the genital area of the nude, but Norman has removed this part of the photograph. Embarrassment? Partly, perhaps. But Norman's further exploration into his own feelings as he talked with us indicated that he did not want to have actual sexual experiences with anyone other than his wife; also, in cutting off the arms, legs, and head from the torso, Norman spoke of realizing that he was not seeking personal involvement with a whole person. All he was doing was going through a period of adolescent curiosity about female sexuality; perhaps he should have worked his way through that long ago but the fact was that he hadn't, so it was time, now, for him to be aware of his left-over morbid fear of being abnormal sexually. The eye accused him. We in the group did not. We paid attention to his dilemma; we supported him with admissions that we hadn't solved all of our own sexual hang-ups, either; we laughed together at our shared absurdities.

The decision to share his worrisome fantasies was Norman's own, based on his need for simple recognition and understanding of a part of his total personality. Bringing this secret behavior out into the openness of graphic forms and words relieved a large part of Norman's tension about being excited by beautiful female bodies; no big worry, just a natural male reaction.

SHADOWED IMAGES

Norman's difficulties in accepting his private and rather furtive sexual fantasies were, of course, related to other problems in his life. The dark flower in his collage was mysterious and rather threatening to him; he couldn't talk about it, he said, because he didn't understand that part of himself. In the group we did not explore the implications of the dark flower. I felt that it was symbolic of Norman's sad, bitter, and sometimes despairing moods, whose roots were too deeply buried and too convoluted to be revealed or discussed in even the most responsive of groups.

About a year after the group sessions ended, Norman's depressions could no longer be ignored by him or by those around him. In a sense, his dark flower's growth covered the whole page of his life. Then he was forced to pay attention to its domination of his feelings. With intense, private psychotherapeutic care, Norman has become more aware of his needs. He continues to work as an art therapist. Although he is actively and empathetically involved in caring for the needs of others, he must still focus on his own struggle of understanding and accepting more of himself.

The most obvious and easily dealt with parts of Norman's collage are concerned with his male sexuality; Coeleen's two paintings (see Plate 4, "Little Black Boy" and "Stretched Out on the Beach") and her writings about them refer to female sexual fears and confusions. In our contemporary culture, most people speak freely about sexuality; we are more likely to flaunt our sexual feelings than to inhibit them. Norman was behind the times in that he looked at his sexual impulses through his mother's Victorian eyes; it took courage for him to expose his thwarted yet natural curiosity and speak of it openly; once he did, that aspect of his personality was less of a problem.

Coeleen has little difficulty with her femininity as far as sex is concerned; she is frankly and openly female in her attitudes and behavior. She is a contemporary woman seeing her sexuality and accepting it as being good within our current social mores. So, though she writes of fears that the "Little Black Boy" will grow into a "dark man" who might rape or seduce her, Coeleen used sexual terms to describe her growing self-assertiveness and her fears that she would sacrifice her femininity to her aggressiveness.

During the previous two years, when her marriage was dissolving, Coeleen had been in individual therapy with a psychiatrist. She needed his guidance because she was facing a life-style very new and foreign to her. As a youngest child, she was considered cute but not very bright. She grew into a lovely young woman, attractive to men but considered more ornamental and amusing than substantial. She married early and well and in quick succession had four children. In a Midwestern town she lived in an elegant home, entertained, was active in church activities, and was told not to bother her pretty head with money or other mundane matters.

Then, when Coeleen was in her mid-thirties, the marriage went to pieces with all the attendant gossip and taking of sides that can happen in a social in-group. The whole miserable scene of accusations, recriminations, and legal battles drove Coeleen into recognizing her own naiveté and then to a determined effort to find her own strengths and wisdom. To do so, she began to explore with her psychiatrist and through her paintings the dark, shadowed images of her repressed anger and aggressiveness. The Little Black Boy symbolized her disowned urges for freedom to explore the wilder parts of her own nature, to risk discovering unmanageable desires and impulses. The telescope, jeweled and elegant, symbolized not only the roles she played but also the self-chosen limiting of her vision to keep her from seeing what she wanted to hide.

Coeleen worked hard; in therapy sessions she dared to explore her shadow side. In living she explored practicalities; she attended workshops, getting experience and training in group leadership; with a male psychologist, she co-led workshops using art as media for developing the creatively feminine in any person. She also went back to school aiming for a Master's degree in educational psychology.

When she came to me, Coeleen was daring large-scale self-explorations. Previously, her paintings had been small, carefully composed, and sometimes overly decorative. The ones done in my studio were huge, almost unmanageable, painted quickly with large brushes and thick acrylic textures; they presented all sorts of ambivalent imagery. I was amazed and sometimes overwhelmed by what Coeleen brought out in her daily sessions. Going down into swirling waters was a recurring theme; so was flying high above the sea with her telescope in hand. The Little Black Boy and his metamorphosis into a mature dark man represented Coeleen's emergence from "the threat of being led astray" by her child-like "knowing but not feeling, sensing but not knowing" attitudes toward reality. The second painting was a climactic and exhausting experience for Coeleen; she had always been treated as a charming little girl; she wanted to grow into being able to assert herself as an adult. In her dream and art imagery, though, she revealed how much she feared doing so. Associating assertiveness with masculinity, she symbolized that latent quality as the Little Black Boy. The little boy part of herself was not reliable, but neither was it threatening; it was only the grown-up adult male emerging as a previously denied part of her personality that frightened and angered Coeleen. She realized that the dark man represented her own strength telling her that she alone was responsible for integrating her adult masculine and feminine sides if she was to be a whole person. When Coeleen writes of being forced "into becoming a woman who could face life as an adult," she is speaking of the inner conflict between her suppressed powerful male side and her little girl side, "kicking and glaring," angry at her own growing pains, even though it is she herself who seeks that growth. She asks herself if she has "what it takes to pursue further."

The answer is yes; since that time, over two years ago, Coeleen has not only managed to maintain a home for her children, she has also made a living leading groups of women in exploring their creative-feminine side and is active in the women's liberation movement. Moreover, she is finishing her second year as a Ph.D. candidate, working for the rehabilitation of women alcoholics, and doing research into their special problems.

No small achievements for a woman presumed to be inadequate in dealing with reality! Her present art forms are large wall hangings made from rug-samples. Rich and luxurious to look at, they show quietness and coherence in composition. Images that had been shadowed are now out in the open.

PERSONAL PERCEPTIONS

It seems incongruous to me for anyone to take for granted that Freud's interpretations in his psychoanalysis of patients in his era are valid impositions on the imagery of people living now in differing cultures. Perhaps there are universals in mankind; certainly we find some behavioral instincts or drives or motivations or whatever we call the common traits we seem to share, but we are not at all sure what is nature's contribution and what is contributed by our society's nurturing. We are living in a time of exploration into the inner workings of human beings; we need to be aware of how we do behave in these times. We need new knowledge to add to the older concepts.

I choose to honor the spirit of Freud's dedicated search but not to honor his findings as universal laws. Freud himself, his family, his friends, and his patients were mostly upper-middle-class Jewish intellectuals and were reared by Victorian ethical, religious, and moral codes. Naturally all of these factors influenced their perceptions and responses to universal experiences. What Freud called infant sexuality has been part of cultures and species older than ours; the young of animals other than man have grown into adulthood in ambivalent relationships with parents and peers. Our myths, histories, and ethnological, ethological, and psychological research attest to our sharing common traits. I assume that our individual behavior and even some of our social behavior has not changed much basically, but our self-consciousness has led us into different perceptions and interpretations.

Even today, cultural backgrounds are so enormously varied that any sort of rigid interpretive code seems inadequate. I would not expect a man sitting on his rooftop while a flooding river washed around him to have the same perception of the word *water* as another man lost in a desert with an empty canteen would; neither would I expect a woman living in a group-marriage commune to respond to the word *penis* in the same way as a sexually frustrated lady living alone would. I can't predict how each would express her personal perceptions, but I'm sure each woman's imagery would be related to her living situation.

Most of the people I know as friends, colleagues, and clients are in living situations quite different from those described by Freud's writings; though quite a few of them are upper-middle-class Jewish intellectuals, their life-styles and goals reflect contemporary conditions. The women do not become hysterical contemplating, remembering, or experiencing sexual contacts (though they may suffer anxiety that no male is available to them for sex). The men mostly seem to have Mother safely in the background and are not fearing Father's castration (though they may suffer anxiety that women's liberation will deprive them of submissive sex partners). We may or may not have healthier attitudes toward sex, but we have certainly grown less inhibited in our sexual expressiveness; we do not hide from exposure to sexual aspects of our relationships with each other, our parents, or our children. In paint and in clay as well as in words, sexual content is depicted openly; the creators of the sexual figures are quite aware of and articulate in using concepts like "penis envy," "castration complex," "oral-anal-genital phase," and so on. Some people grow eloquent and go into great detail; sometimes I wonder what's underneath the facile sexual-hang-up diagnoses. Could it be that we've gone full circle and are using glib and easy Freudian terminology to avoid rougher anxious realities? I am not intimidated by sexual problems in the art forms; I just find it a bit absurd to go snooping around for covert sexual symbols when overt ones are so fully displayed.

SENSORY MEMORIES

What is overtly displayed does not necessarily tell the whole story. Sometimes the persons creating art forms consciously disguise content; often they use symbols to stand for more than is obvious; more often they're only partially aware of the full import of their expressions.

All of us know about repression and suppression of disowned emotions and thoughts; we know that talking and verbal free-associating sometimes make us aware of ideas and feelings long hidden. We use such therapeutic approaches in art experiences and know the value of verbal recall. But I think non-verbal activity is far more effective in bringing into awareness some memories that do not respond to words. For lack of a more concise term, I call these sensory memories.

We all have sensations in the present that seem to be related to past sense experiences. Hearing a snatch of a melody, we might feel nostalgic; sights, smells, tastes, movements, colors seem familiar but somehow out of context. When we can't connect the sensation with any event or even with an actuality we can name, we puzzle a bit, but since present sensations obscure past ones, we forget even the half-formed sensory memory. Most of the time, getting in touch with these ephemeral sensings serves only to satisfy our curiosity and enrich our memories, but sometimes our wordless, irrational responses to sensate stimuli become so compelling that we need to examine them with our senses for the sake of our reason.

This is where non-verbal therapeutic techniques are especially valuable; sensory memories are best aroused through sensory experiences. People who can't or won't put their undercover sensations into words often do so when they have gotten in touch with them through awakening experiences of body-awareness, movement exercises, psychodrama, and the using of actual materials to enliven the senses.

In the gestalt art experience we use our sense perceptions and trust them to lead us intelligently. We pay attention to sights, sounds, textures, and movements that we create; we recognize the individual ways that we perceive and interpret similar sensory stimulation. Sometimes we can trace the variation in individuals' responses to sensory stimuli to a difference in their initial experiences in the past with the same stimuli.

To simplify by caricature, let's create a pair of twins, Jim and Joe. They grow up together in the same home, are equally healthy, smart, loved, and so on. As adults, they still look alike but they behave quite differently. Jim is a jolly, extroverted fellow, smokes big cigars, drinks a lot, loves the outdoors, has many friends, and becomes a forest ranger. Joe is a secretive, introverted guy, hates cigars, is a teetotaler, never goes outside, has few friends, is always worrying, and becomes a janitor. From a common background, how did Joe and Jim grow to be so different?

I invent past events that influenced each. When Joe and Jim were 9, the family planned a weekend camping trip. Just as they were about to leave, alcoholic Uncle Ed called, moaned that he was suffering from gout, couldn't walk, and begged that one of the boys stay with him. Joe and Jim drew straws, and Joe lost and was confined to Uncle Ed's apartment for the weekend instead of going out into the woods. Uncle Ed was an ornery cuss, drank whiskey straight, and fell asleep in his chair, leaving a stinking cigar smouldering in an ashtray. Joe, in his misery, sneaked a swig of the whiskey and felt nauseated and dizzy. He emptied the ashtray into the garbage can under the sink and dozed off on the couch, feeling fuzzy and sorry for himself. He awoke smelling something burning, sniffed a bit, and decided it must be Uncle Ed's cigar. He remembered dumping it. He saw smoke coming from the kitchen. Dashing there, he heard the crackle of flames and opened the cabinet; the flames flared out, and he burned his hands pulling out the garbage can. The smell was terrible when he doused the fire with water. He put it out, though, lugged the can out, emptied it, and cleaned up the mess. Besotted Uncle Ed still snored and Joe had no one to talk with. He kept the whole incident to himself, never spoke of it, and eventually forgot it; but when he's exposed to either the taste of alcohol, the smell of smoke, the sight of flames, or the sound of fire crackling, or feeling hot, he feels disgusted and guilty. He clams up; since he does not consciously remember the incident, he has no way of discussing his sensory memories.

Jim has different sensory memories. On the camping trip, his father smoked cigars (they smelled great in the open air) and drank some brandy (even gave Jim a taste to warm his gullet); the smoke from the fire smelled delicious; the hot coals warmed his backside; and he went to sleep feeling content with himself and his world. Jim, too, has forgotten the events of that weekend but his sensory memories remain, and today he chooses similar contentments.

All of us have sensory memories connected with happenings we've forgotten and perhaps suppressed. Fortunately no one incident of the kind I've just described determines our stance in life. In order to account for the different personalities of Joe and Jim in real life, I would have to ask and answer many questions about their genetics (were they identical twins or not?), their earlier experiences (was Joe one of those people who seemed to attract trouble?), and how it happened that Joe could not talk about his trauma. To make this story believable, I'd have to fabricate far more complex personal histories for the two boys. To keep the example simple, I omit imagined sequences of how Joe's experiences continued to reinforce his expectancy that he was ill-fated and how he retreated more and more into secrecy and fear of others; his over-reaction to alcohol, smoke, heat, and fire then would become the outward manifestations of stored-up anxiety.

I would also have to postulate that Jim was unusually lucky that nothing overly traumatic had happened in his life; perhaps I could imagine that Jim was so satisfied with the camping trip and the easy companionship that he never experienced fear of aloneness.

Obviously the process of personality development is not this simplistic and we usually don't find such easy contrasts in real life, although I've known some to be as clear-cut. A middle-aged woman, Sarah, in a week-long group program repeatedly painted areas a soft, faded blue and spoke of that color representing terror. I know that people have personal color codes but soft blue is usually used for "spirituality," "serenity," "free skies," and such qualities. Sarah insisted she sensed terror with blue, so we encouraged her to keep trying to get in touch with her memories. Toward the end of the week she painted a large human figure all in blue and in doing so she remembered. When she was 2 years old, her parents went to China as missionaries. She was put in the care of Chinese nurses who dressed in soft blue pants and robes; she'd forgotten the actual events of when and what but remembered that she associated that color and the terror of being abandoned. None of us in the group could have told Sarah how to interpret her feelings; she found out for herself by using her sensory memory.

Sarah's discovery did not in itself change her life drastically. She was a social worker, closely involved with others, and her aversion for blue did not interfere with her capabilities; however, in becoming aware of the feelings of being helpless and abandoned evoked by her blue-clad figure, Sarah reached deeper into unresolved emotions. She pondered and talked with us about how she still could not maintain a mature relationship with her parents; though she was an adult in most situations and quite capable of taking care of herself, she was still haunted at times by an ephemeral fear that her elderly parents had the power to destroy her self-assurance by deserting her. In paying attention to this childish fear, Sarah was able to understand herself better and to recognize how she could better cope with her irrational fears.

Sarah experienced a process of getting into contact with her feelings by communicating with paint and words. In doing so she became aware of some sensory memories that she couldn't understand; when she gave her attention to her puzzling responses, she got in touch with imagery of her early childhood, imagery that she'd kept secret even from herself. With her personal perceptions of what emotions she'd held back, Sarah interpreted her own symbols (blue representing terror) as they had evolved from her unique experience.

Chapter Five

GIVING AND RECEIVING MESSAGES

SEEING WHOLE

Sometimes we understand each other intuitively—we exchange a few words, touch together, or maybe make contact only with our eyes. Surely we are communicating! That's beautiful when it happens. But sometimes we try to reach each other in all sorts of ways and give and get only confused messages that result in no contact or communication at all. What's happened to our intuitive powers? Can we rely on such an elusive sense of knowing that excludes conscious reasoning? Does intuition exist at all?

I think it does. Sometimes I know without knowing how I know; so do most people. Without these subtle but sure perceptions we would not be nearly as wise as we are. But I don't think intuition is either a miracle or a skill that anyone can acquire in 10 easy lessons. Intuitive understanding grows with experience in perceiving honestly and reasonably the millions of nuances in life's realities; our perceptions of meaningful relationships help us develop confidence in our intuition. But sometimes we see only details and parts and have no idea of how they are or could be related. That's when a conscious mind comes in handy: when our intuitive insights fail us, we can use our mind to observe and reason our way to some conclusion that helps us function.

In the gestalt art experience, we create things made from materials; in themselves, they have no particular meaning; the way we perceive them makes them meaningful. Since these are the creations of unique individuals and are seen by other unique individuals, how can we hope to find any common ground for communication? If we don't intuitively understand each other's imagery or have a system of definitions common to all imagery, how can we begin to comprehend messages between us?

To answer these questions, I go back to the gestalt notion that the whole is more than the sum of its parts. Applying this concept to learning better ways of communicating, I say that we can practice envisioning the total process of a person creating art forms; in seeing the whole we learn that our latent capacity for seeing the relationships of the parts comes into play naturally. When we concentrate on the total gestalt, we perceive how the differences and similarities of the details form patterns to which we respond without labored reasoning. Intuitive understanding, then, becomes active as we learn to stretch our vision wide enough to include many possible views of the meaning in any message.

When we are adults who have been conditioned by our culture, stretching the vision of our mind's-eye often means that we must free ourselves from habitually narrow vision. If we are to see more widely we must stop looking from only one viewpoint; we can see all of the facets of a form only by moving around to see from all sides; limiting ourselves to one perspective is likely to distort the whole image.

Of course, there are many kinds of perspectives; we use them according to what kind of picture we want. Since in gestalt art experience we want to see the whole person, we use as wide a range of perceptions as we can muster. It is impossible to say where one way of perceiving ends and another begins, and there's no easy dictum for interpretive processes. I suggest we interpret art work by guiding our intuition to focus on: the life style that everyone brings to the experience and how he carries that style into his art work; the literal and symbolic content in specific works and how this may appear in other forms in a sequence of works; the media the person chooses for expression and how these media are manipulated; and, most important, how the creator interprets with form, actions, and words what he perceives as his message.

LIFE AND ART STYLES

Whether we know it or not, we are each our own stylist; style is a subtle and always distinguishing quality. It is "that certain something" that everybody has but nobody can define. Style is the essence of personality shining through every action. Life styles are reflected in art styles, and often we can see in art works stylistic qualities that are not easily perceived in living. In pictorial representations we see style aspects always in conjunction with aspects of content and media. In art experience when we want to be aware of the whole process, we do not and cannot separate these aspects either in creation or interpretation; they all work together in getting across their total message.

In order to learn how we use style in manipulating media for presenting content, let's look at several creations and focus on their style and the life style of the people in process who created them.

Cyndy's two drawings (see "I Want," Plate 2, and "Perhaps Tomorrow," Plate 3) were done four years apart but I see in them similarities in pictorial style; I also see that her way of living is reflected in her way of drawing. Cyndy's drawings are curvilinear, informal, energetic, and the lines move fast and free. The loose forms, unfettered and unconfined by boundaries, are centered in the space. But the figures rest on no base and are without background. The words in Cyndy's poems express the same touch-and-go mobility. In her living, Cyndy's actions show flexibility, quick changes of viewpoint, and restlessness in physical and psychological movement. Her moods and attitudes shift in a way that is sometimes disconcerting, but she is not evasive and she does not get lost in trivia. She's directly head-on in relationships with clients and therapists.

Cyndy's habit of not drawing backgrounds or bases for her figures indicates to me that she does not feel enclosed or supported in her personal life. She leaves spaces for free movement—she wants personal freedom. But the tentative, delicate beginnings of background in "Perhaps Tomorrow" and the tone of the poem express Cyndy's ambivalence about wanting both freedom and security. She did the first drawing, "I Want," with brash, unblended lines; in "Perhaps Tomorrow" she pauses, covering and merging some lines with care.

Helen's style contrasts with Cyndy's in both living and painting. Helen always begins a painting by creating a background; her figures grow out of solidity; they emerge as she experiences. Helen's life style, too, is characterized by wariness, caution, and introspective considering before she risks direct statements and actions. Once she's sure, she's very sure; her "Autumn Tree" (Figure 5) and "Monster Man" (Plate 1) stand centered and sure, clearly defined against the background. In "Moods" (Plate 2), figure and ground are not so clearly delineated, nor did Helen exercise so much control. Though she still planned ahead, intending to paint "the whole sheet of paper black, black, black," she recognized her changing mood and allowed the bright colors to flow in random paths.

In living, now, Helen allows more and controls less. She still must have her solid ground behind her but can let figures emerge and become part of her wholeness with less fearfulness.

Cyndy and Helen—both mature, active professional women who are effective in their work with others' problems—show different styles in dealing with their own problems. They differ also in what kind of representations they choose for their drawings and paintings. Cyndy draws her inner organismic feelings; Helen projects hers onto outside objects when she paints.

CONTENT

The actual images in any art creation are its most obvious content, but its total message cannot be discerned without referring to the total context of the images—the style in which they're portrayed, the relationships between figures, the choice of emphasis in depiction, and, quite often, what has been left out of the picture. I cannot provide any reliable structure for interpreting art; there are too many variables in the individual, cultural, and psychological experience of the creator. In order to make sense out of such messages, we must always consider the widest possible gamut of expression aspects.

Pictorial expression includes both the range of actual subject matter, as wide as the world of visible objects, and the gamut of kinesthetic and emotional experiences, which are more felt than seen; also, graphic communication is often presented entirely through symbols that stand for ideas that are neither seen nor felt. Keeping all this in mind when we want to grasp the full measure of art forms is not easy; grasping and claiming the one and only truth of a message is obviously impossible. But we must begin somewhere, and figure content is the easiest aspect to perceive.

The people whose processes I've chosen to write about have a tendency toward abstraction; my choice reflects my opinion that often people can and do present a more focused and clarified message when they abstract from literal likenesses the element of immediate relevancy —the figure in the background of appearances and situations. For instance, in "Monster Man," Helen could have drawn a literally represented background for the figure, but she was not concerned with environment, as such, so she abstracted the man's surroundings into simple planes of color and texture. In Helen's "Moods," she could have painted a landscape—water, sky, and trees—but she was most interested in mood content.

Going back for another look at "Monster Man," it is obvious that Helen is describing more than an emotional mood. She is using the figure to convey some specific attitudes and opinions about men, so she paints a man with no equivocation. The figure appears starkly and uncompromisingly on center stage, but his stance is awkward and impotent, he has no feet to stand on, no hands to touch with, and his arms hang suspended from rigid and exaggeratedly wide shoulders, joined to a narrow caved-in chest. The ridiculously small penis between wide-spraddled legs and the corkscrew hair complete a picture of Helen's acknowledged contempt for the overbearing, threatening aspects of masculinity.

Fortunately for Helen and for the men who are her friends, the content of this painting is more a catharsis of long-hidden feelings than it is a statement of Helen's overall attitudes in relating to men socially and professionally. The content here must be interpreted in the context of Helen's life style and recognizing her changing thought and mood patterns as she becomes more aware of her inner self.

Cyndy, in both of her drawings, is focusing on her inner aware-ness of felt frustrations and desires. The first drawing, "I Want," sug-gests a female torso, but Cyndy has only sketchily indicated a head, and she ignores arms and legs entirely. Cyndy has abstracted from a total female figure those parts that she feels she is "trying to squeeze open," trying to make tomorrow happen now. The torso, though curvi-linear, suggests constriction and containment; the green outlining strokes inclose impatiently: wanting, trying, squeezing, burning, and feeling closed are the contents of Cyndy's drawing; the half-form of a woman is only a vehicle used for focusing on organismic awareness.

In "Perhaps Tomorrow," Cyndy's abstract shapes convey to me movement up, around, and out, repeatedly twisting lines into a loop, leaving a negative space as the center. Cyndy draws all around it but neither with lines nor words does she go into the "something exciting, upsetting, delightful, scary, ecstatic, evil there." She wants "to stay away right now." Perhaps tomorrow Cyndy will explore that "yellow-white center." The content of this drawing, then, is an abstract descrip-tion of Cyndy's movements around an area of awareness in herself.

The gestalt art experience, with its emphasis on being aware of how we perceive our inner reality rather than how we see the outer actuality, naturally elicits introspective imagery. Since images are created from experiences of fantasizing and realizing, those chosen for any graphic message are influenced by both the nature and nurture of any individual. The content of any one form depends on the present life situation of the person creating the form. In a series of pictures and sculpture by one person, though, we can see patterns of what kind of images each chooses for conveying content. Norman tends toward realistic representation; Helen is inclined to select material from visual reality to express her hidden emotions; Cyndy relates body states and movement to content; Coeleen is more likely to use symbols, often drawn from Jungian sources, to portray her concerns. Celia and Sharon, both artists, are prone to exploit the art materials themselves as a con-text for content; for them, the media is an important part of the message.

MEDIA AND EXPRESSION

In using the graphic language, we want to create visible forms that are congruent with our inner imagery; we want to express graphically how we are thinking and feeling. Inevitably, we will do this in our own style, and the content we include will reflect what is happening in our lives at the time. To translate how and what we sense from inner subjective realms to outer objective forms, we use art materials. The kinds of materials we use then become an integral part of the art experience; the media contribute to or distract from the completeness of the visual message.

Different personalities discover which art media seem most natural to them. Professional artists and those experienced in using art materials find that some media are more congenial than others; though they may be knowledgeable about and skillful in many media techniques, they are usually most expressive with only a few of them. The same is true for people who are untrained and unskilled but who are using art media for personal expression. They, too, feel more comfortable using some materials than others. Given time for experimentation and some minimal guidance, each person can discover his perferred medium. But, obviously, the materials must be available for such experimentation!

I realize that it is not always possible for therapists to provide the time and materials so a client can experiment. I regret the necessity of sometimes limiting the scope of art experience to a session or two, during which the client's attitudes are evaluated on the basis of a few quickly done drawings. I am wary of giving an opinion or even interpreting art forms unless I can see a series done over a period of time and with various materials. I have observed too often that people who seem completely blocked in expression in one media will freely create imagery with other materials.

For instance, the widely used scribble technique reveals how a person sees forms or can form some pattern in a tangle of self-created lines; that revelation may be significant. But someone may not be accustomed to perceiving forms in two-dimensional, linear, colorless scribbles. Such a person sees the scribble but it makes no sense to him in terms of experience; give this person clay to manipulate and he may be able to create coherent forms that belie his confusion in scribbling. I observe that men, especially those who use their hands in making three-dimensional objects, can become perceptually blind when they are asked to make something out of a small, one-plane scribble. I've seen dancers and athletes—who ordinarily use their whole motor system—grow awkward, frustrated, and immobile when they try to draw something small using only hand and arm motions. Given large surfaces and broad tools to paint with, they get their whole body into what they're doing.

Some people are intimidated by blank surfaces; they fear desecrating a clean, open space and put their imprint on it only if they're forced to. For these people I suggest collage; the cutout shapes can be placed on the paper tentatively and removed immediately. That option removes the timid soul's fear that he "might make a mistake and ruin the whole thing." The shapes can be moved around on the background by the experimenting artist until he feels secure enough to paste them down.

As people become acquainted with art media, they can and do choose the materials and tools most appropriate for representing their feeling states. Celia, an accomplished artist, works in many media; the two examples of her work demonstrate how different materials, themselves, help to convey different messages. In "Inside Myself" (Plate 3), Celia used felt-tip pens; the square felt tip dragged the color onto the paper, slowing down the curving lines. To get solid color areas, Celia had to fill in the spaces, painstakingly going over and over one spot. The media itself restricts movement to mostly the wrist and hand. The hard-edged color areas require concentration, an appropriate way of depicting "Inside Myself."

Celia painted "All Over the Place" (Plate 4) in a mood of happy abandon; she chose a 40" × 60" sheet of rough paper, a wide-splayed brush, and vivid primary colors. With these materials the colors, lines, and shapes flowed fast; Celia was actively involved, with her whole body moving about the painting while it lay on the floor. She literally was "All Over the Place."

Sharon, too, uses various media, but her two-dimensional forms always seem too tight for her. She prefers three-dimensional forms with obvious edges that can be touched (see Figures 6, 7, 8, and 9). She also likes the quality of being able to see the form from many angles. She writes:

> I want to communicate who I am and how I feel in the most honest way I can, but I also want the courage to exercise my imagination and extend my illusions to encompass all the intricate feelings I enjoy and relate these to other people. I enjoy finding the order and possibilities innate in disparate objects, as I am now beginning to find the order and possibilities innate in myself. I am interested in the interrelatedness and juxtaposition of shapes and objects. My meaning is derived from looking at myself in juxtaposition with others; I enjoy rearranging objects to find a comfortable composition that I can look at and live

with. The more time I spend exploring the space I have created, the more I find things are meaningful to me.

My own preferred media is different from Sharon's: I like textures, especially those of organic forms, so I create them with layers upon layers of acrylic impasto. Then I scratch and scrape through the thicknesses and discover what's underneath. I'm sure this says something about my wanting to get down to what seems essential to me.

In art experience, I want everyone to explore and express what is essential to him. I want everyone to find his own best medium for expression. That's why I'm always watching for art messages.

Part Three

USING THE
GESTALT ART EXPERIENCE
FOR YOURSELF

Chapter Six

DOING *WHAT* COMES NATURALLY

MAKING YOUR MARK

One day I was walking along the ocean. There was no one else there, so I claimed the place as my own and sat down, being pleasantly lulled into mindlessness. Then, on a point above me, I saw that someone had been there earlier and had left a work of art for anyone to see. On the reddest of the clay shelves that paralleled the water were placed two large white oval stones. The artist had smoothed the ground around them, had scratched radiating lines in the clay, and had placed one stone atop the other in perfect alignment with the curves of the clay shelf. I had no idea who had crafted the clean beauty of that structure and can only guess what it meant to him, but I do know that he was using art materials to structure something of his own.

A young friend of mine is making a quilt. She can afford to buy any blanket or ready-made spread, but she is fascinated by making designs that are uniquely hers.

Dave is an engineer who can earn a handsome salary working for construction firms. Instead, he looks for jobs working with wood—designing furniture as he makes it and constructing wooden frames and shelves that are both useful and beautiful. He insists on doing them his own way.

Marvin is a psychologist who uses all sorts of art materials to express what he is feeling when his intellectual vocabulary fails him. He also plays very serious games with himself, using cutout colored shapes as symbols to help him see, literally, the configurations he is forming of the actual elements of his living patterns. On a wall of his apartment, he has pinned a variety of abstract shapes in various colors and sizes. The whole wall is a mural with parts whose interrelationships he can change to suit his mood. Sometimes bright colors predominate, and on some days somber darks cover the wall. Marvin never plans what the effect will turn out to be; he just moves the shapes around until the arrangement seems congruent to him, and only then does he interpret the message of his visual imagery. One evening in my studio he spent several hours alone working with cardboard, white paint, wooden blocks, and wet red clay. Later, he brought his construction into the house and talked quietly of its significance to him. On the cardboard box were vertical blocks of wood, starkly white. Among them were long coils of sinuous clay. "You see," Marvin said, "the worms are crawling through our present civilization. They are destroying the cold unfeeling edifices we build so high. But the worms are not our enemies; they are destructive only in that they are changing what must be changed so we can build other structures more suitable for humanity's basic needs." In his professional life, Marvin uses his intelligence with precision and decisiveness, but when he involves himself with art materials, he intuitively formulates wordless comprehensions that are beyond exactness.

Last year I was in love, an old habit I keep falling into. I cared very much for a man who cared very little for me. He did something that I thought abominable. I called him up and let go with all the vituperative words I could muster, then hung up, feeling self-righteously vindicated. Still I was frustrated and could not sleep. My mind kept chattering on about how wronged I felt, and there was no one around to listen to me except me, so my inner dialogue gave me no release. In a temper, I started spraying and throwing acrylic paints onto a large sheet of cardboard. Orange, red, white, and black were all running together and forming tangles of shapes. I saw a face—my face—in one of the blotchy puddles of paint, and I began to develop the image. For several hours I was totally involved with the colors and webs of lines, letting them take the forms of my emotional confusion. Finally, I knew I had made myself clear. I looked at my own image-making, chuckling at my absurdity, empathizing with my childishly hurt pride. I made explicit both anger and hurt and could then let go of my conflict of loving and hating at the same time. Physically exhausted and emotionally rested, I went to sleep. The next day, when I showed the man my painting, he said he received my total message much more clearly than he had from my fury of words.

Thirty years ago when I was young and artistically snobbish, I would not have called the stone and dirt arrangement, the quilt, Dave's woodwork, Marvin's constructions, or my emotional outburst in paints ART. Like many other art students, I was a devotee of the fine arts, unabashedly agreeing with my fellows that we, the talented and serious professionals, knew what art was. Looking down our disdainful noses at crafts and illustrations, we were in awe of ourselves. Art was special, and only the specially endowed could create it. Art was for its own sake and lost status when it was used for decoration or illustration. Insistently we claimed we were purists and muttered resentfully about dilettantes playing around with art materials without our soulful dedication. Over countless cups of coffee, we wondered who among us would become great.

Now, after many years of being and living with people who are called artists, and after many years of knowing others who make no claims of being especially dedicated but who nonetheless create through the media, I am not brash enough to categorize.

I am brash enough, though, to say that art is not only a medium for self-expression, it is also a way of extending the scope of experience that is available to all of us. The professional artist with his sincere dedication and developed skill can execute his art work masterfully. Some of this work speaks of universalities; some portrays the cultural milieu of the artist; some expresses the inner perceptions of the artist; some will endure in time; and some will be ignored and forgotten. For those who dedicate their lives to the specialized field of professional art, I feel respect and empathy.

For craftsmen, trained and untrained, I feel appreciation and admiration. They transform objects from the merely functional into a statement of the craftsman's aesthetic awareness and skill. Thus they doubly enrich our lives.

Those who use art as a mode of experience—for fun, for making something decorative, for creating something of their own, for expressing something of their inner lives, and for therapeutic release—are taking an equally valid and important approach. They use the same media and materials as the professional artist and craftsman.

These approaches to art are not mutually exclusive; I use art in all these ways, and so do many people. Let's put aside the categorizing that is not relevant to art as a personal experience. Let's use art to make us more aware of ourselves as psychic and social beings.

Like Marshall McLuhan, I see art as "more than ever a means of training perception and judgment."[1] I agree with him when he says, "art offered as a commodity rather than as a means of training perception is as ludicrous and snobbish as always."[2]

I want to eliminate that snobbishness that prevents many people from using art. So, I want to stress that art materials need be no more complicated or esoteric than sticks with which to scratch lines, knives with which to carve wood, clay with which to model a form,

[1] Marshall McLuhan, *Understanding Media: The Extensions of Man* (New York: McGraw-Hill, 1964), p. ix.
[2] *Ibid.,* p. x.

stones with which to build edifices, paints with which to cover a canvas, and a piece of chalk with which anyone can make his mark.

GUIDELINES

I would like to suggest some guidelines that will help you get the most from the gestalt art experience. The guidelines are actually articles of faith in the human potential for self-discovery, authenticity, and creative autonomy. They apply to you no matter what your background, education, occupation, status, or age may be.

1. Trust your perception of what is right for you. Rely on your body, mind, and spirit—your whole self—to give you an awareness of what you are. Listen to others, hear what they say, and then accept as true only what seems valid to you. You are not infallible, you do make errors, but you are your own best authority.

2. Know that you are in process and you cannot remain static; you are always changing, always growing. You have many alternative ways of growing—some ways are better than others, and you can choose some alternatives and refuse others. Be honest with yourself and realistic in recognizing your possibilities as well as your limitations.

3. Respect your own kind of creativity as being natural for you; don't contrast or even compare your way as being better or worse than that of another. Do your own thing, let the other do his; respect each other's uniqueness; more often than not, you will find communalities between you.

4. Let yourself get involved; do not deprive yourself of immediate experience by thinking you already know what will happen if you do participate. Use your good sense in saying no, but don't let your preconceptions stop you from saying yes sometimes.

5. Give yourself permission to play and be foolish. You may be surprised at how much you can learn by chance while you are playing.

6. Be aware that you are aware. You are continually sensing, thinking, and feeling. As a living organism in any environment, you are always interacting with your surroundings and with yourself. The more aware you can be of the process taking place, the more you can choose what you want to happen.

7. Accept response-ability as an enlivening adventure instead of a deadening obligation. As long as you live, you cannot possibly be passive; as long as your heart beats and your lungs draw breath, you are inevitably active. What kind of activity is best for you? You are responsible for choosing from what is available.

8.   Re-cognize your perceptions. Real-ize your excitement; actual-ize your potential.

9.   Don't aim for ideal goals that you might attain in the future. Concentrate on the reality of how you are living in the ever-present now.

I add another testament of my belief:

You can:	Be more how you want to be, Do more what you want to do, Move more where you want to move
When you can:	Know and accept how, what, and where you are now.
You can:	Have genuine contact and communication with others outside you
When you can:	Contact and communicate with the complexities within you.
You can:	Live more fully in the complexities of the world around you
When you can:	Give full attention to the simplicities directly perceived by you.

So the way to go about reaching splendid goals is to forget about the never-never land of idealistic achievement aims; let your energy flow into the reality space of what is available to you here and now. The basic formula for you to follow is simple: You + experience + awareness = increased potential for more and better applications of the same formula toward the most and best for you. You don't have to change the world; as a matter of fact, you can't change the world without changing yourself, and you can't even change yourself, basically, until you take some time to discover the interwoven pattern of personality that is the real you.

So you start with self-exploration, seeking self-discovery; you map out your own course; you are in charge of your own safari; you choose guides if you need to, follow them as you want to, but when in doubt about your best direction, consult your personal compass.

Right now, I am assuming the role of your guide, suggesting how you can begin to move according to the indications of your compass' pointing. Paradoxically, I tell you that if you want to go on a self-exploration journey, your first step is not to move in any direction at all; since you are both the explorer and the explored, it is important that you have a good sense of your present position and orientation before you move from the familiar you into areas that may seem strange and foreign to you.

BEGIN WHERE YOU ARE

You can begin right where you are. How do you feel right now? Most people answer automatically, "fine," "lousy," "tired," "happy," "miserable," and with other generalized words. Try, instead, to be aware of some actual body sensations. Are you comfortable? Warm? Cold? Hurting? Hungry? Thirsty? How are you feeling in the position you are in right now? Relaxed? Tensed? Want to curl up or stretch out? Wiggle your toes. How does that feel? Most people never feel their feet until they get corns and complain. What's going on in your stomach? How's your breathing? Are your teeth clenched or resting freely? How about your jaws, your eyes, your lips? How are your hands feeling? Move them around a bit, letting yourself do with your hands whatever you feel like doing. Move the movable parts of your body, and pay full attention to your movements. After as many awareness exercises as you care to do, ask yourself again: "How am I feeling? See how much more you can say in response. Listen to yourself and find out how much of your bodily feeling states you can get in touch with before reading on.

Figure 10 shows some quick drawings done by a woman who obviously wasn't feeling good.

Now, use your body's senses to get in touch with you in your present environment. Feel yourself in contact with whatever surface you are sitting or lying or standing on. Touch other things and concentrate on your tactile sensations; see things around you, listen to the sounds, smell whatever is smellable, and maybe do some tasting, too. Make your environment real to you by contacting whatever is around you through your own sensations.

Doing this sort of sensitivity awareness exercise is basic to any kind of immediate experiencing of being you in your environment at any time, no matter what you are doing. Maybe you are one of the few people who already do this anyway. Many people are so busy thinking about the past and the future, remembering and expecting, that they seldom sense fully what is happening in their immediate present. I suggest that you take time to live the present moment and continue this practice whenever you find yourself dwelling on "I used to be," "I wish I were," "when I become," "some day I will," and so on.

There are many ways you can bring yourself into direct contact with what you are feeling and thinking now. One of them is to make drawings that express your present perceptions; you can use your hands to create concrete representations; you can use your vision to bring into focus some thoughts and emotions that seem to elude you when you cannot express them openly. When you do this, you are using an age-old and universal language.

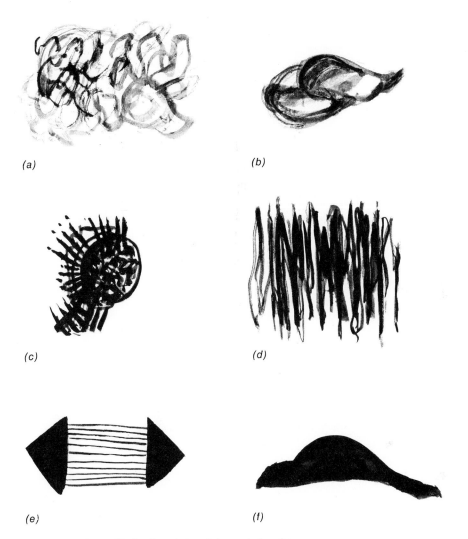

Figure 10. Feeling states: (a) sweaty hands;
(b) soft insides; (c) headache; (d) wet throat;
(e) tight mouth; and (f) heavy body.

USING THE ART LANGUAGE

When we think and talk and write about language, we usually mean verbal language. Naturally! We humans learned to talk thousands of years ago, and we haven't stopped doing it since. We learned to write words and to reproduce them with printing; then we found we could send words through wires and via the air. So now wherever people are found, words are, too. Of course!

You and I go to the beach. We listen to the wave's sound. Then somebody walks by with a transistor radio going full blast. We drive up a mountain road to see the scenery, and right where we don't want it to be, there's a billboard with printed words ten feet high telling us to buy something or other. We hear some beautiful music and, while we listen, we say words to each other. We become aware of the wonder of the night sky, and we try to put our awe into verbal language.

So that's us—Homo sapiens, knowing so much and using words to tell each other what we know; wanting to comprehend and trusting verbalization as our best means to that end; longing to be understood and expressing that need in words.

Now I write my book and add one hundred thousand words to those already in print. So that's me, too, hoping that I can use words to tell you that there are ways to communicate without words; I am verbalizing about a nonverbal language.

I can write all about nonverbal art experience and you can read what I write, but you won't know the reality of what you can experience with art unless you use the materials in your own way and for yourself.

You can all do this, but some of you don't know you can. You are familiar with verbal language, so you use words without much embarrassment. But you are unfamiliar with art materials, so you approach them warily. You think art is for specially talented people and for kindergarten kids. Since you are neither, you say you can't use art for you, except by looking at the art made by other people.

I say you can use art experiencing for yourself if you want. Using pictorial language is as natural to you as verbal language is. If you say you can't make pictures, I tell you that you can, you have, and you do.

You draw signs and symbols when you write notes; you make maps for others to find directions; you draw sketches when you want to show somebody something, and you doodle. You use the language of art comfortably and naturally so long as you don't call what you're doing *art.*

So forget the word *art;* pick up a pencil, a pen, a crayon, some house paint, or anything that will make marks; find something to make marks on; then make your own marks. Scribble, doodle, or make forms. Don't try to do art. Don't expect to make a representation of anything in particular unless you want to. Find out how you want to draw, and what you want to draw. Do how and what seems natural to you.

Forget your first-grade teacher who told you to do a pretty valentine for Mother; forget those miserly coloring books where you had to stay inside the line; forget your mother's "But, dear, what is it a picture of?"; forget that art course you had to take in high school, when the teacher had cold plaster models of Greek sculpture that you were supposed to render with smudgy charcoal. Forget all your failures in drawing and all your triumphs in copying. Most of all, forget your own judgment of your talent or lack of it. Forget the markings you make now, or at least don't study and analyze them to death. Pile them away somewhere while they're still alive and warm, and go on making others to add to the pile.

If you are particularly reticent about your markings, you can become a secret agent in your own investigation of a new language. You are a businessman—realistic, sober, and practical. Though you've always had a secret yen to play around with color, you've always been too inhibited to do it openly. Makes you seem absurd, childish, effete. Doesn't fit your image. Your colleagues would tease you. Your wife would be indulgent. You'd feel silly.

All right, so be silly! Let drawing be your secret sinning. Sneak down to the corner drugstore and buy a set of felt-tip watercolor pens and a large pack of typing paper. Tell the curious that you have to make some diagrams. Okay, so make some diagrams, and let them be of whatever you want them to be. Maybe you'll have to start with words, so draw words—tough words, tender words, ugly words, poetic words. Draw all the words you are feeling—sex, sadness, play, despair. Make the words big, little, plain, fancy, and use different colors for different words. What color is *sex* for you? What color is *sad*? Find out for you. Then maybe you will want to draw what your chosen words mean to you. Stop drawing the word and draw your feelings.

You can do that any way you want to. Your graphic language can be created by you as you go along. It is your language, and you don't have to learn it from anyone else. You say what you want to, too, and you can keep your expressions all your own as long as you want to. Maybe you will want to share them with others, maybe not. That's your choice. The important thing is that you're using another language and expressing yourself in a way that gives you something you want.

DOODLING

You may be inhibited by the word *drawing,* so use *doodling* instead. Get some paper and pencil and doodle. Don't try to draw a picture; just let your hand move around making any kind of lines that come naturally. Follow your lines with your eyes, but don't interpret or judge them; just go with what you're doing. Stop reading this now, and cover some pages with your own doodles.

I collect doodles—other people's and mine. Some of them appear in Figures 11 through 15. Don't look at them until you have some of your own to see.

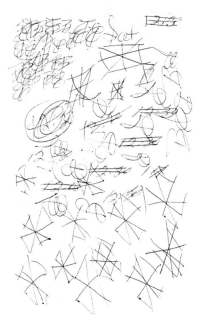

Figure 11. A schoolteacher doodles her weariness.

Figure 12. Doodle by a secretary who is impatient with her job.

Figure 13. The doodles of a girl in love.

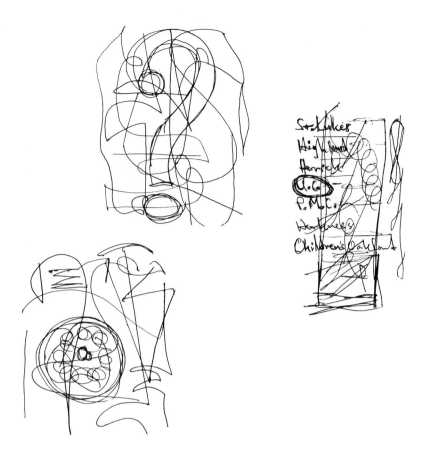

Figure 14. A doctor doodles.

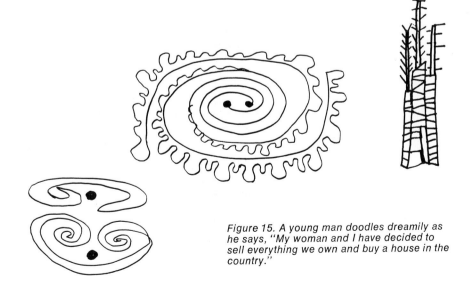

Figure 15. A young man doodles dreamily as he says, "My woman and I have decided to sell everything we own and buy a house in the country."

If you make a lot of doodles, experimenting with the different kinds of lines and shapes you can make with pencils, pens, and crayons, you may want to buy yourself a "doodle diary." I recommend a spiral notebook that is small enough for you to carry around in pocket or purse and inconspicuous enough for you to bring out during boring meetings, while watching television shows that don't interest you, during those interminable waits in reception rooms, during conversations when the other fellow is long-winded, and when you are alone wishing you weren't. Draw as you feel like drawing without giving conscious thought or attaching any particular meaning to what you are doing. When you've finished one page, go on to the next. At some point you will thumb through your doodle diary; you may be surprised to find continuity of themes or maybe obvious changes in the way you are using lines and shapes. Perhaps you'll gain some insight into what sort of messages you're giving yourself. Your doodles, of course, are self-expressions, and you are using symbols as representations of something that is part of your thinking and feeling.

SYMBOLS

So how about playing around consciously with graphic symbols? Draw some combination of lines that seems to portray how you are feeling. Something simple like: "I'm feeling great—like I'm on top of the world"; "I'm feeling confused. I'll never straighten out the mess I'm in"; or "I feel like I'm flying high." Play a game with yourself; draw your symbol in several ways, discovering as you do which ways come closest to being a succinct visual metaphor for your emotional states.

You have been using symbols as means of communication for many years without necessarily knowing that you do. Certainly you read signals and signs that are not words but convey to you a message that can be translated verbally. You drive your car, responding to simple shapes painted on highway signs; you react to the changing colors of traffic lights and the turn signals of other vehicles. You recognize various religious and societal symbols and are influenced by trademarks of organizations and businesses. Figure 16 shows some common symbols. Nations, political groups, clubs, and some families design symbols to represent themselves as they feel they are; they create some simple graphic image that identifies them.

You can do the same for yourself; in making up symbols of your self-identity, you can have fun, find out more about your self-image, and learn how to use your visual perception as a medium for self-exploration. A pack of 3″ × 5″ plain index cards, something to draw with, and your own ingenuity is all you need to start with. Draw one

Figure 16. Some common symbols we all
recognize.

symbol for you on each card; keep the drawings simple and straightforward; don't take time to explain the symbols or elaborate on them
until you've made as many kinds of designs as your imagination suggests to you. To help your image-making, pause between drawing on

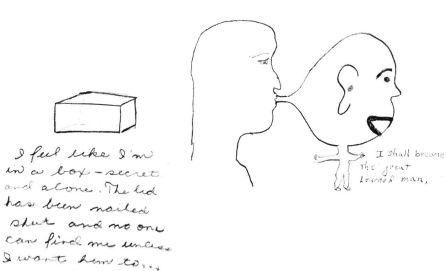

*I feel like I'm
in a box - secret
and alone. The lid
has been nailed
shut and no one
can find me unless
I want him to...*

*I shall become
the great
learned man,*

*Most of me I'm saving
just for me - I'm starting
to let in people only
where I want them - I'm
secure inside me for now.*

*my cringing, barbed self +
my super-shiny, brilliant star of
the conversation -
the shit they protect +
my childish fears
an arrow pointing in to what
I can't see -
There's too much of me I
don't like —*

Figure 17. "I Feel."

the cards, close your eyes, and listen to yourself in words. You may be thinking something like, "I feel like a king," "I'm nothing but a blob," "I'm going in all directions," "I feel flattened out," "I feel tall and strong." See Figure 17 for examples of this kind of doodling.

I feel Like a beautiful yellow and black butterfly near a wild flower free and blithe — alone in my solitude

I am a gigantic, inert blob !!!

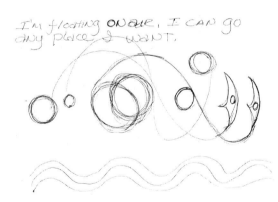

I'm floating ON AIR, I CAN go any place I WANT.

God! How many me's out of Touch with me's —

Some of your doodles may appear on your cards; some of your symbols may not be yours originally. No matter; you're doing this for your own experience, not for showing off to the world.

When you've made as many cards as you want, spread them out on the table or floor; arrange them in relationships and sequences that seem relevant to you. Eliminate those that you do not identify with; change the symbols if you feel inclined to. Select the cards you feel identify you best; recognize the ones that represent aspects of you that you don't like. Do anything you want with your symbol cards; they're your "Me-cards," to be used by you, for you. My guess is that you can shuffle through them, thinking, "I'm quite an interesting assortment of traits. I'm worth spending some time with!"

ANIMATING YOURSELF

Now that you have discovered that you can make marks, scribbles, doodles and symbols to represent your feelings, your thoughts, and your identity as a person, how about taking a next step? Animate some of your qualities in the form of a story using comic strips and film cartoon techniques. As we all know, comic strips and cartoons are not necessarily funny. Some beautifully potent and serious messages are contained in the simple presentation of a series of drawings that depicts characters moving through experiences.

In this experiment, make yourself the central character in a drama that can be absurd, poignant, tragic, or maybe just a simple picture story of something that is happening in your life. This self-animation experience is deceptively simple: although the materials and techniques are simplistic, complexity and subtlety result from your infinitely varied and changeable personality. You can do extraordinary things with an ordinary pencil and paper. I know this is true because I've seen it happen so often.

To produce this picture-story, choose the setting, the roles, and become the director; but let the script unfold as you go along; let the sequences develop from one drawing to the next; let the outcome of the story evolve as you perceive it would in reality.

You can use your index cards or your doodle diary, but mostly use your imagination and your free-flowing acceptance of the sort of childlike playing around with images that you may do until you discover images that make sense for you. Remind yourself again that there is no right way or wrong way for you to draw; there is only your way. It doesn't matter if your drawing makes no sense to anyone else. The important thing is that it have meaning for you.

Figures 18, 19, and 20 show sequences drawn by three people. None of them has had art training or has ever done this kind of thing before. Each chose his own symbols and an individual concern to portray. These are excerpts from "to be continued" strips.

Dorothy, divorced and being determinedly cheerful, began by choosing a star vaunting her freedom (see Figure 18).

1. I am a star in the sky; feeling free, shining, and bright.

2. I feel uneasy up here all unsupported. I find that I am a falling star.

3. I land on the sea and enjoy floating around on the surface like a starfish.

4. My tentacles get weak and droopy. I feel myself sinking. I'm afraid.

5. I try to crawl around on the sea bottom, but the currents push me around.

6. I find a rock and cling to it. I need something solid to hold onto.

Figure 18. Dorothy's cartoon.

After she drew her cartoon, Dorothy burst into words. "Hey! Now I know! I'm just not the type to be a career woman. I want to be married and have some rock-bottom security." She hasn't found a husband yet, but she knows what she wants and is keeping her eyes open for a likely candidate.

Dennis, who teaches literature in a university, sees himself as a tragicomic figure (see Figure 19).

In other drawings Dennis depicts himself as a gladiator, as Hamlet, and as Don Quixote. The lines he draws across his face become a helmet, a mask, or a riveted robot head; in each facial covering, there is a slit through which he peers at the world. Through art and other experiences, Dennis is discovering how he has limited his vision and how he confuses sorrow, anger, and his need for support.

Gene, an educator with an intellectual bent, prefers celestial symbols to express his very real inner conflict (see Figure 20).

Gene's tough, hard-shelled, masculine crescent and his tender, soft-exterior female oval are both authentic aspects of his personality; each trait is wary of the other, but he is being most genuinely himself when he can accept both as valid and mutually supportive.

Like some movie and newspaper cartoons—"Peanuts," "Pogo," and "Feiffer,"—the cartoons of Dorothy, Dennis, and Gene contain humor and pathos. We all experience both in our daily living; sometimes we can comprehend a complicated life drama better when we can separate the whole production into a series of incidents. Sometimes, too, we can get a better perspective on truly serious involvements when we can laugh or at least smile with ourselves at what wondrous fools we mortals can be.

Whether or not you can solve anything with your cartoon strips, you can at least animate your recognition of the daily to-be-continued nature of your living. That is an important step in learning how to write your own script of the day-to-day process in which you are the central character.

Before reading further, try it for yourself and see how your study progresses.

Figures 18, 19, and 20 showed events in a linear sequence, as if the realizations followed each other single file. Actually things usually do not proceed in such orderly fashion, nor does a person come to terms so tidily with one behavior trait while his other characteristics stay passive and non-interfering. Usually you live a complex existence that calls into play a whole range of emotions and thoughts that activate each other in a cluttered and sometimes unnerving fashion. When you are in the midst of such an interplay, you realize that you are feeling and doing a lot of different things all mixed up together. In order to make any sense out of your confusion, you must first recognize that none of you is a simple one-dimensional figure. Each of you is a configuration made up of the multiple interweavings of your many personal

1. Since my wife's death, I am sad and suffering.

2. I am keeping one hand on my heart and holding my suffering in the other.

3. My sad cross is pointed; I am angry at the doctors and at myself because my wife died.

4. I want to punish somebody for something, so I take my cross/sword in my right hand.

5. My sword is not very adequate. I don't know what to do with it.

6. I want to fight against all violence and death, but I need something to lean on. I am confused.

Figure 19. Dennis's cartoon.

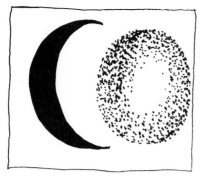

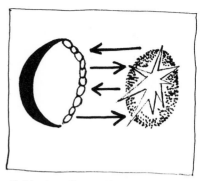

1. My polarities are a crescent, clearly defined but hard and empty, and a soft oval that could fill the crescent's emptiness.

2. I try to pull myself together and see that my crescent part has a hard wall outside and my oval a cutting wheel inside.

3. As I meet myself, my two protective systems clash in mutual destructiveness. Neither part of me trusts the other.

4. So I back off from myself to engage in two-way objective examination and evaluation.

5. I decide that both sides of me will have to give up part of their defensive barriers; cautiously, I move my opposites closer.

6. I know that I am not perfectly integrated; however, I am less alienated from myself and can function better as a whole.

Figure 20. Gene's cartoon.

qualities. In order to function fully, you must realize how interwoven and interdependent are the parts that make up your identity as a whole.

You can illustrate this by taking simple figures that represent parts of your personality and putting them together in relation to each other so that you do or do not come out with a total configuration that seems structurally sound to you. Before you do, look back at the strips done by Dorothy, Dennis, and Gene; each of them recognizes some unfulfilled need in his life.

Dorothy wants the solidity of a rock's support; she thinks a husband would fill that need. She may have to provide her own security by developing her own rocklike qualities. If she can do this, she can keep herself from being washed around by the currents and not be too dependent on a man doing it for her. Then, if a husband comes along, he can be an extra bonus for her, not just a filler-in for her weaknesses.

Dennis knows that his wife's death left him without someone to lean on. His loss and consequent sorrow are genuine, but he has put on a mask to hide his feelings of resentment; he has assumed a role of passive suffering that is self-immobilizing. In accepting his confusion about the role of his sword, he is now facing his genuine human needs instead of posing as a dramatic character out of a book.

Gene, though his figures are nearly abstract, is aware of his two-sidedness and of his imperfect integration. Knowing fully how self-destructive his hardness and his softness can be, he accepts himself as he is; thus he can make realistic choices as to what he can and cannot do. (Though Gene showed only two figures in relationship, you could draw many more than that and put them together.)

If you identify with the simple shapes and lines that have been used to show these personal configurations, then use them in your own drawings and add others if you like. Perhaps you'd prefer more literal representations that have more meaning for you. For instance, you could choose some fairly universal symbols like snakes, hearts, birds, animals, stars, knives, skulls, flowers, or hundreds of others. With your awareness of what each figure means to you and using your own inventiveness, you can make innumerable combinations. Perhaps your graphics will help you realize some situations you put yourself into. You may even get some clues about how to get yourself out of dilemmas or how to enjoy more good states of being. At least you can gain insights into why and how you play games with yourself.

You know that you are a complicated configuration of traits, that your moods vary continuously, and that you are sometimes bewildered by your complex individuality. You know that every other person, no matter how different he may be from you, is also a complex personality who is probably going through all sorts of mood changes in himself at the same time you are. And when two of you are interacting, especially when you live interdependently, things can get into such a muddle that you both despair of ever straightening out your temperamental tangles.

We all live in some kind of grouping—families, communities, organizations of all sorts. Most of us are involved in several groups at the same time, and these groups are related to other groups, and so on and on. The scope of even trying to comprehend the networks of interrelationships existing among the people I know personally stuns me; trying to understand the infinite extension of that network into any larger dimension stupefies me.

So I come back to a premise on which I base my philosophy and work: person-to-person contact and communication is the keystone for supporting any sort of structure! Any configuration—whether it is a solar system, a machine, a personality, or a group of people—can function best when each part of the whole fulfills its role in whatever activity is taking place. I don't know much about solar systems or machines, but I do know a lot of people, and I am concerned that we cooperate toward creating the best possible whole we can.

One of the parts I play in this total process is to suggest how you can use simple devices like scribbling, doodling, and symbolizing for increased contact and communication with yourself and others. How about showing your expressions to some others? How about several of you doing some drawing together? You can have fun, enjoy your differences as well as your likenesses, and get closer to each other in understanding and acceptance.

Chapter Seven

KNOWING YOURSELF BETTER

INVADING YOUR OWN PRIVACY

I can verbalize my feelings, thinkings, and imaginings. I can act out the dreams and dramas I create privately. I can play with, paint, and model objects that show my personal fantasies, both representational and abstract. As these words, acts, and graphic expressions become explicit, concrete, and observable by others, I am communicating with art some of the forms of my inner experience.

We know that all the messages we send and receive are incomplete; we give clues to each other. With our gestures, words, and symbols, we show traces of our inner lives. We usually interpret only part of each other's messages. But if we share common experiences and trust our intuition, we can perceive nuances not concretely expressed. When we also care for each other and love enough to want to understand, we sometimes reach a completeness of communication that defies explanation in any logical terms.

In art as in life, this complete understanding evolves through personal perceptiveness. If we want to reach each other through art forms, we must each contribute willingness and openness to see and be seen as we are. The art forms exist on their own as things; you and I create and endow them with meaning. If we want to touch each other meaningfully and complete our mutual acceptance of each other's uniqueness, we must let go of the defensive barriers that confine and defeat our inherent yearning to perceive the whole even when some of the parts seem to be missing.

The missing parts are often hiding behind walls of fear. When I do not trust you, I fear that you may destroy what is most intimately mine, and I build a protective wall around what I want to keep private; you do this, too. So we hide ourselves from others, spending time and energy to maintain our barriers, desperately patching our cracks with conformity and bracing our weak parts with self-righteous indignation. After a while, wall-maintenance becomes habitual, then compulsive. Sometimes we actually forget what it is we are trying to hide. We have barricaded off some parts of ourselves so successfully that we can't even invade our own privacy.

So, we no longer have access to our own wholeness. Being alienated from ourselves, we cannot completely be with others. We come together socially, we make safe conversation, ask polite questions, give careful answers. Sometimes we feel a vague sense of loss and sadness, wondering without words why we are so alienated from each other.

Using art experience to reach behind our walls and make images of the feelings we have disowned is a way of alleviating alienation from ourselves. Visualizing our fears can reduce their hold on us; drawing a picture of a long-hidden ghost can help us look at it without flinching. When we can perceive the ghost, we can accept or deny that it is a part of ourselves, but at least we are getting in touch with some of the long-hidden self-images that keep us alienated from our totality. When we can invade our private cache of disclaimed emotions, can claim what is truly our own, then we can bring to any relationship a fuller sense of being what we are and can choose to risk more genuine contact with others. We can withdraw into our privacy, too, when we choose to and not because we are forced to by compulsive fears of being exposed.

If you are willing to invade your own privacy, if you want to make concrete visual images of what may be behind the façade you show to the world, I can suggest ways you can do that with art media.

First, let go of any preconceptions of what kind of images you might make; it is possible that you are a wolf in sheep's clothing; it is possible that you hide your sheepishness behind wolf's clothing. It is also possible that you are not in disguise at all! Maybe you really are what you seem to be. But do you know how you seem to others? Most important, do you know what kind of image you have of yourself?

Most people don't. A look in the mirror will give you information you already have anyway. Also, you can describe yourself somewhat objectively, giving data like age, sex, height, weight, coloring, occupation, income, and that inevitable social security number. We are all asked to fill out forms that supposedly describe who we are but that often reduce us to nothing more than just another statistic in somebody's files.

Yet we don't perceive ourselves as just a card in a file of other cards; we perceive ourselves as unique. And we are!

MOVING WITH YOUR DIRECTION

You can discover much about your perception of yourself and your sense of personal identity when you stop mentally filling in the forms someone else imposes on you. Let your own self-created, unique forms emerge; the data your forms present need not make sense, even to yourself. In art experience, you can relax, stop thinking of how you should think, and let happen what will.

Before we get into the experience itself, let's look at the word *should,* one of the most powerful words in our culture. It's a word that we have heard since childhood and that we hear constantly as adults. It's so pervasive that we each seem to have a *should* computer impinging on our every movement and thought. *Should* is that evasive fantasy of what is right for every situation.

Fantasizing about situations can be a very productive and creative activity. It's most productive and creative when it's your own fantasy, not your expectations of what someone else's fantasy must be like or your fears of what will happen if you don't do as you should.

Shoulds ("I should have done this," or "I should do that") inevitably are not creative fantasies about either the future or the past. In using art, you will be actively in the present, and there's just no room for *shoulds* in the present.

For a letting-go of *shoulds,* put a stack of paper in front of you, have plenty of colored pens, crayons, or chalks nearby. Then begin with no goal except that of making strokes that express how you feel. Do not draw a picture of anything. Make lots of lines on lots of pieces of paper. Don't be stingy with your materials or your involvement. Try making all sorts of lines; experiment with finding out which kind feels right for you. Make angry lines, scared lines, nervous lines, happy lines, excited lines, loving lines. Which kind feels right for you? When you find one sort of stroke that seems to express you right then, repeat that same sort of stroke a number of times, varying its qualities as you want to. Try different colors and see which ones you identify with the most. Don't stop and ponder, though; just make strokes with one color and then with another; use your lines and colors like instruments in an orchestra; let your hand improvise variations on a theme. In this case, there is no score and no conductor; you are improvising your own music.

As your strokes become surer, you will probably find you are drawing rhythmically; let your body—your hands, arms, shoulders—move with that rhythm; move as much as you can with your own beat, and do not stop drawing your lines. Begin emphasizing your rhythm with some sounds that seem to belong with your movements and your drawing strokes; try different sounds until you find your own—perhaps a drum's beat, a banshee's cry, an owl's hoot, a mourner's keen, a baby's wail, a cowboy's whoop, a worker's grunt, a child's whimper, a lion's roar, a boy's whistle, a cantor's chant, or a bee's murmur. Try any sound that resonates inside you. Let your voice, for once, find your full range of expression; let your body find your range of expression; leave your drawn lines and move with your whole self, the kinds of motions you were making with your lines: flowing, jerking, going around and around, jumping about, zig-zagging, pounding, whirling, wavering, jiggling, going straight, trailing listlessly, curving gently.

When you have found your own synthesis of sound and movement, rest among the clutter of line drawings, and now allow yourself some time to ponder.

Let your pondering be about how you expressed yourself with movement and direction. We use our sense of direction to tell us how we can get where we want to go; our kinesthetic sensing tells us we are moving our bodies. But often in ordinary situations we ignore our direction and movement and the messages we are giving out and taking in via body language. Most of us have settled for a limited repertoire of body language; we are, literally and figuratively, muscle-bound. We bind ourselves with habit, propriety, embarrassment, fear of letting go, and our assumption that movement should always be directed toward a rational goal. This exercise is one for getting you out of the bind you rationalize yourself into when you harness your natural body activities and drive toward a goal that may not be sensible for you.

To assimilate your experiences in this exercise, start with the lines you made on the sheets of paper; concentrate on the directions you moved on the page; remember the rhythms of your body movement and how your sounds followed the movement of your lines and of your whole body. Consider your voice an instrument for making audible some internal emotional movements that you feel inside but seldom let out full-throatedly; realize that vocal cords can be used not only for speech; they are also a part of you that can vibrate with a wide repertoire of moving sounds.

So, in this project, you can experience concurrently and synchronize drawing, moving, and sounding; you can explore how you direct your movements when you have no goal other than to discover more of your own identity.

CREATING YOUR OWN IMAGE

In setting forth to move with your direction, you may have become more aware of the movement qualities you can express with your hands, your whole body, and with the timbre of your voice; however, you were advised not to make a visual image of yourself. At best, you had a stack of paper with colored lines to refer to, and, more important, you developed a kinesthetic sense of synchronizing various modes of expressing yourself in motion.

Now I suggest that you incorporate some of your kinesthetic sense into creating a clay image of how you perceive yourself. Again, I say, before you begin, put aside as well as you can any concepts of how you should be, how you fear you are, how you want to be; especially do not think of how others see you and what you see when you look into a mirror.

To do this, put your trust into your hands; let your energy flow into them; take as much clay as your hands feel like holding; sit quietly for a while, holding your clay in your hands; close your eyes and become quiescent and receptive to your inner self. Feel the malleability of the clay. It is passive in nature; your hands are active. Let the activity of your hands mold the clay experimentally; explore how you can change the shape and surface of the clay—squeeze, smash, smooth, break, gouge, tear, puncture, roughen, caress. Don't judge your actions: neither force nor restrain them—just feel what you are feeling. Then go into a fantasy, a dream state, a game—whatever is best for you—and say to yourself subvocally, "This lump of clay is me. I am creating myself." Keep your eyes closed and stay with your feelings; sense through your hands how you can symbolically express with the clay what you do to yourself in reality. If you sense shapes and textures that evoke emotional awareness of realness in what you are doing, continue that pattern of molding; if you feel that an image is emerging, change your subvocal chanting to "This is me. I am." Let your image change and grow as you sense its rightness for you. When you want to, open your eyes and contact your image with your eyes. Figure 21 shows five self-images created through the experience.

Stay in contact with your vision and your touch and any emotional resonances between your imagery and yourself. Trust your intuition in receiving the message you have made visible and concrete; allow yourself some time and quiet for contemplation; let your interpretations come to you through your senses of sight, touch, and your associations of symbols to reality. Don't try to fit your interpretations into any system used by others. You don't have to be systematic or explanatory. It is enough if you can accept your self-created image with the simple awareness of "This is me. I am."

If you are with others and want to speak with them of your experience and of your image, do this with the same simplicity of description; if you do not want to use words, let the seeing of your image be enough for you as well as for others.

This introspective kind of art experience can be a form of meditation. It is not necessary that you carry it further, but people often want to. For me and for many others, the creation of our own images is a way of getting in touch with our feelings of self-identity, and we use the images often as referents in communicating with each other; they act as bridges among us, making natural and easy some exchanges of confidences that would be very difficult without the presence of the

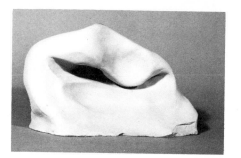

Figure 21. Five expressions of "This Is Me."

image—an image that fills in so many of the gaps that words cannot express.

Sometimes I suggest that people create a self-image including two messages: one, "This is the me I want to share with you"; and two, "This is the me I want to keep private." The two aspects can be combined into one figure or made into different forms. Sometimes people literally hide the private image inside, behind, or under something! Usually, there is no need for such precautions, though; when someone says of his image, "This is the private me," we accept his wishes and do not pry. Often the image-maker volunteers a clue or two of his own accord, then a little more information, and soon it becomes obvious that the creator was kidding either himself or us! Obviously the privacy-image represents what he was most anxious to make public! That's all right with us. We all have our little ruses for getting attention!

Another revealing way of using this technique is to make two entirely separate images: one, "This is me as I feel in relationship with a primary other in my life"; and two, "This is that other as I perceive him to be." Some very angry imagery appears in this project; some beautifully loving imagery emerges, too. Naturally, the image-maker often perceives and represents some of his own unacceptable traits as belonging to the "primary other." When this is made explicit in the clay and in words, the originator can often recognize his own projections.

Figure 22 shows a twosome made by a young woman, Claire, who felt both fondness and frustration toward her nondirective psychotherapist. Claire describes her feelings:

> This is me talking to my shrink! I'm pale and twisting around but I feel defiant enough to wave my hand derisively at him. He just sits there, not telling me anything about himself. All he shows me is a formless façade. He won't share with me whatever goes on behind his professional front. So I have to imagine; this is what I project onto him.

Figure 22. "Me and My Shrink."

The backside of the therapist's image, shown in Figure 23, was an undulation of shapes all intertwined—ideas? complexes? worms? Claire took the image to her next appointment with her "shrink." She reported only that he laughed. Soon afterward, though, they terminated the therapy sessions with mutual consent and goodwill.

Figure 23. "Backside."

Some people are not aware that they project themselves onto others; in fact, I have known persons who seem to have no sense of their own individuality as separate from that of others; if they have, they do not express it in their imagery. Sometimes a person will appear completely absorbed in creating "This is me. I am." imagery; then he will show an assortment of figures and say, "This is my wife, this is my mother and father, these are my children, . . ." and so on. When asked, "But where are you?" he will answer something like, "But of course they are all part of me," or "I am in all of them." When I receive a message like that, I find myself at a loss, but I keep trying. I suggest that the participant put aside his other figures while he does a "This is me" image of the part of himself that is in relationship with those others.

I feel even more at a loss when people create an image and say, "This is not me. This is the world, and I am not in it."

Here are approximate quotes of how seven persons gave this message, disowning not only their self-identity but also denying that they had any part in the world.

    1.   A middle-aged woman, frustrated in her efforts toward social reform: "This is the world, flat with mountains like walls around it. There is no way out. It's hopeless. No place for me in it."

    2.   A black teen-ager, both hostile and gleeful: "Here is the world, like a big firecracker, like a rocket; it's going to explode and kill everybody. I'm not going to light the fuse; nobody is. It'll just go off by itself and blow everything to pieces."

    3.   A woman who is a psychiatric social worker, weary and defensive: "The world is a planet with no life on it. It's covered with sharp, pointed peaks. I'm a little speck in there, but I have no life, either."

    4.   A man who is a sculptor: "This is the world—a smooth perfection of movement, going around in undulating curves. I could do many pleasant things in this world, but right now I am not in it."

    5.   A harassed physician, angry with his many responsibilities: "I make a world like a rolltop desk in which I put things I can't do anything about and lock them up. I lock myself in there, too."

    6.   A shy young girl: "The world has all these funny shapes, piled up on top of each other and not making any sense. I'm safer not being in the world. There might be an earthquake."

    7.   A bearded young mystic: "The world is perfectly round and conical with universal love at its highest point. I am not in the world as an individual since I have transcended my ego boundaries."

    All seven were participants in gestalt art therapy groups, but fortunately each was in a different session. Had all of these statements come out in any one session, the group would have been totally frustrated in any kind of interaction. How could any of us communicate with the world if none of us considered ourselves part of it? How could we respond to someone who spoke only of a depersonalized world? How could we have dialogue with someone who disclaimed any identity in the group?

    The mystic didn't seem to want a response; he sat smugly in the yoga position, transcending. The young black dared anyone to contradict him; no one did!

    The others seemed to be asking for answers; at least they wanted some sort of reaction from the group. In portraying their feelings of isolation, they were sending out a covert SOS. Usually this message elicited a variety of responses, ranging from sympathetic tears to fuming anger, which resulted in intense interaction among the other group members that eventually involved the isolates themselves. Often the process of admitting that you are closed off can open doors you didn't know were there. Using the medium of clay is wondrously effective in bringing out into the open all sorts of half-realized emotions; with your sensitive hands you can feel the clay and form it into images with visible qualities.

Get some clay, at least 25 pounds; try your hand with it and see how you do. You may be very surprised at what you can create out of damp earth.

When you are creating an image of yourself with clay, you can actually touch and mold this stuff of the earth. You can sensually feel the image emerging. When I do that I enjoy feeling the shape and dimensions of my image; I do very little thinking then.

But I don't live only as a sensing organism; this me that molds the clay is also being molded by the passage of my life-time.

YOU IN YOUR LIFE-TIME

The abstract dimensions of time are beyond my comprehension. I can play intellectual games with myself, trying to conceive of what time is; although I enjoy my speculations, they set me awhirling and I come back to where I started from: time is, time was, time will be, and I must live the changing me within the seemingly unchanging dimension of time. So, I come back from my speculative journey in abstract realms and re-enter the tangible world of experiencing my perception of time with art media.

One of the most interesting art forms related to the idea of time perception is to use a roll of paper and make a sort of scroll on which you paint your perception of time. The roll of paper can be of any size that you choose. You can buy rolls of rice paper, shelf paper, or wrapping paper in many widths and textures. If possible, get several widths and give some attention to the size that seems right for you. For working on the paper, I suggest you use opaque water colors because you can paint over areas if you want to. Have several sizes of brushes and jars of water nearby. Perhaps you will need a roll of Scotch tape, too, in case you want to add some more time-space to work in or patch up places where you go to pieces. You may want some scissors and glue so you can move a depicted event in your life-scroll from one time area to another. Besides this, all you need is a willingness to concentrate on your lifetime, or life-time—think about the difference. How do you live in it?

Before you begin painting, I suggest you relax your body and let your fantasies wander around in your life-time perceptions. We speak of time as being divided into past, present, and future; in discussing events, both historical and personal, this tripartite division is certainly convenient. However, in our subjective feelings and thinkings we frequently are not sure whether we are living past memories in the present or trying to deal with our future anticipations as if they were actual now. We become confused! Before you start on the paper scroll, unroll your mental and emotional notions about how you are relating your individual past, present, and future time.

Then take your paper and unroll as much of it as you feel you want to portray your life-time on. Be aware, as you roll out the paper, that it has a linear dimension, just as time does. In actual time you begin your existence, of course, in the past, and you are now in the present, journeying into the future. In the art experience, you are free to tamper with time's linearity; you can start in the middle with two rolled-up ends; you can cut it up into segments; you can cautiously leave the roll mostly coiled up and feel your way into slowly finding out how much symbolic time you want to explore. Also, you can start painting your future and/or your present first and paint your past next; or you can paint in all the areas a little bit at a time; or don't separate the time sequences at all; or leave out any time that you feel is not important to you; or you can ignore all my suggestions and do whatever you please.

You are in your own life-time! You have the privilege and the responsibility for claiming and being and doing in your own life-space. Once when I was drawing my sense of time, I grew impatient with my own directions. I rebelled against my conceptions that time is a continuum from then to there—or vice versa. I said to myself, "Right now I am not aware of past or future. I am aware of being here, temporally present, in warm contentment; at another level, I am aware that I am a tiny speck existing in eternal, infinite time." Without explaining my awareness at all, I ignored my roll of paper and did the two quick sketches shown in Figures 24 and 25.

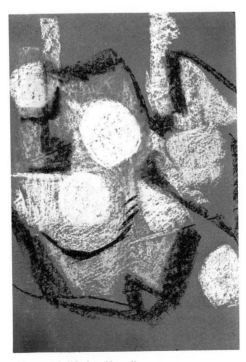

Figure 24. "Being Here."

Figure 25. "Tiny Speck."

In my studio, a young woman did a painting of her life-time on a 4-foot-wide roll of paper of which she covered 60 feet before she stopped from exhaustion after three hours of splashing on gallons of poster paint. She never paused to consider any areas, she didn't do any interpreting in words except once, when she said, "Oh, good! Now I'm putting some people into my life!" She was very young, a professional dancer, and she was pregnant.

A man and a woman painted their life-times on the same paper, side by side, but not going into each other's space (see Figure 26). She, on the left side, began at the top wtih her past and went down to her future. He, on the right, moved upward into his future. Just above the mid-point, in present time, they almost touched—but not quite.

Once when I proposed this art project to a group composed mostly of faculty members in a California university, I didn't know that one of the participants was a man who taught and wrote conceptualizations about time. After he did the drawing, we laughed together as we explored our different approaches to clarifying attitudes toward time. He gave me a small book he had published. I was fascinated with what I read, although I knew I hadn't the vocabulary to comprehend many of the concepts he wrote about. His art vocabulary wasn't very sophisticated, either, but he was pleased with his drawing (see Figure 27) and wrote about it as follows:

Figure 26. "Woman and Man."

Figure 27. "Vertigo."

I found the exercise most difficult to begin, for I had spent months, perhaps more than a year, reading, thinking, then writing about time. In my written work, simultaneity, synchronicity, and the fracturing of linear conceptions of Time were celebrated as liberating, even heroic. Process was all, or almost all; the narrative gave way to the total moment, and causality in the traditional sense was cast aside in favor of continuous flow or pulsation.

Yet my drawing of my own life-time appears to have given the show away. What I see there, and what I sensed while at work on it, is the comfort I feel with both past and future time, seen as a continuum, and the disorientation I experience in the immediate moment. Twenty-eight life-times (of threescore and ten each) since the birth of Christ, eighty since the dawn of Jewish history—and all in an unbroken line. There I stand at the center, sucking up with my evolutionary and historical vacuum cleaner the lessons of the past, the triumphs and failures of men. In the distant future lies . . . nothing much worth worrying about. My children, triangles of green, orange, and blue, become the repositories of impulses discharged by me and by each other.

The center of disorientation, of disorder, is the immediate moment. My vertigo is perhaps best depicted in the leaning tower and in the bewildering bombardment of impulses from the past, the future, and from myself to myself. As I looked at the whole for the first time, this was my thought: no wonder I celebrate the heroism of process without form, time as immediacy; by so doing I both tame that process and invite others to take their places with me in this fearful domain. Come one, come all, and don't forget the bread and wine!

Martin

Martin is a man in the middle of his life-time, in his mid-forties. He has a responsible position as an engineer in a large corporation. He does his work well, yet he wants to free himself to choose and do his own thing. In his personal life, he is the middleman between the two people most closely involved in his life but who oppose each other through him; his vitality is pushed inward by his own conflicting personality traits—one side of him demands constraint, while the other strives for spontaneity.

In his drawings and with words in our ongoing group, he visualizes and verbalizes himself as being held on the middle ground of inaction while his two "kings" issue contrary commands from opposite sides of his nature.

Though Martin is in the middle, he is not crushed into a nonentity; with his strong sense of personal identity, with his confused but viable desire for finding his own best place for being, he is making progress in integrating his polarities.

During the last few months, he has made 60 drawings, one a day, mostly during his lunch hour at his office; he munches Fritos and spends that hour drawing and coming to terms with himself as he is—in the middle of his life-time.

Martin has found his own way of using drawing to express how he is living in his life-time and gain insight into it. Until three months ago, the idea of using crayons and paper to make simple drawings of how he was thinking and feeling seemed a waste of time to him. Nonetheless, he followed a suggestion and found so much in it for himself that now he has devised his own program and every day makes a drawing, spends time exploring what messages he is giving himself, and writes in a journal what meanings and movements he sees daily: a self-motivated man, he is creating a chronicle of his here-and-now recognitions, which naturally evoke memories of his past and suggest possibilities for his future. Here are Martin's words:

These drawings are a journey into myself. They are an attempt to become familiar with and understand a part of me I have long ignored. I began with some doubt. I no longer have any doubt. My journey is exciting, frightening, interesting, and enlightening. I am pressing on.

1. (See Figure 28.) I am confused by what I find in myself. There is no clear direction. I have several centers that are sources of confusion. Some are now active, some are not. Some of it is frightening, some of it is not. I hold it all.

2. (See Figure 29.) I bring order to the confusion. I apply constraints. My success is doubtful. Things are still not clear; my feelings still seem blurred and mixed to me. They do not fit neatly together. My constraints seem to be failing and are themselves mixed, as my feelings, drives, desires are.

3. (See Figure 30.) I want to hold on to the people nearest to me. I want to hold on to the conflicting persons I seem to find within me. I feel that I cannot hold both but

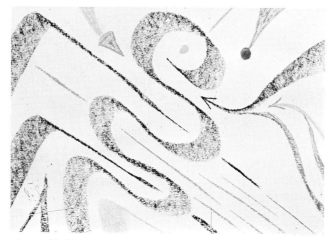

Figure 28. "So Much So Fast."

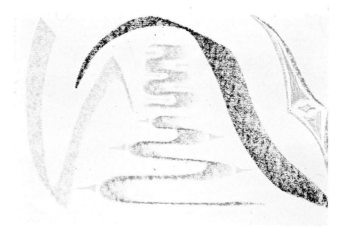

Figure 29. "Try Reordering."

Figure 30. "Held In."

must choose one or the other. I do not want to make a choice. Both of the people mean so much to me. Both of the persons I seem to be are valuable to me. I freeze into inaction.

4. (See Figure 31.) I assert my inner authority. I command myself to action. I command myself to make the order I feel is necessary. My force of command leaves no room for anything else. It is meant to smother all resistance.

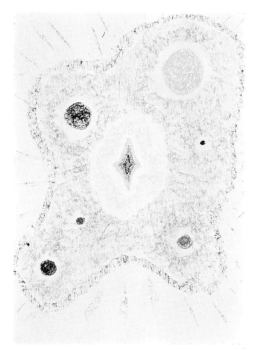

Figure 31. "New-Whole-In."

Figure 32. "Having It Out."

Figure 33. "All Come Together."

5.   (See Figure 32.) My constraints are looser and softer. They will not fail so easily. They will give a little. My feelings are more distinct. They are all still there and have room to change. I have more freedom. I can move more easily by myself. I see things more clearly.

6.   (See Figure 33.) I see my life, I see myself. I stand between the two sets of demands I impose on or ask of myself. I am two persons. One wants to impose order and assert authority, demanding rationality, consistency, and precision. The other asks for freedom to be what I am, to allow things to happen as they will, to take risks, all self-allowed and accepted. I ask myself how I can live like this, how much of a life is possible, and how much of myself I am squeezing out of the picture. Must I be one or the other, or can I reconcile the two?

From my initial confusion through my discovery of two different mes to my feelings of where I stand, I have found my journey into myself most productive. I am surprised at the variety and wealth of things I have found. I would not have believed it if I had not done it. I am continuing, intrigued by the prospect of what more I will find, hopeful of discovering even more of myself, of learning who and what I really am.

Obviously, there are many varied, intriguing ways to portray ourselves living our life-times.

Find your own way.

Chapter Eight

LIVING WITH OTHERS

SPACE TO BE YOURSELF IN

Just as we all have our own attitudes toward time and how we live in the span of it that is ours, so, too, we have our individual feelings about having space to be ourselves in. Whether or not we are conscious of it, we each react negatively when we sense that we are attempting to be who we are in a kind of spatial dimension that is not fitted to our needs; the old saying, "You can't fit a square peg into a round hole" expresses a dilemma we often get into. We don't have to decide whether a square peg is better or worse than a round one, nor do we have to judge the merits of a round or square hole. But if we imagine ourselves as pegs and our space as holes, we can function together better if we consider what shape we are in relationship to the space around us.

Of course, there are times when we must reshape ourselves to fit into certain situations and times when we can't do so and have to make do as misfits, at least temporarily. But it is possible that each of us can find or make a kind of space that we fit into very nicely without major alterations if we take some time to pay attention to what our spatial needs actually are; unless we have some notion of what kind of space we are looking for, though, we won't be likely to recognize what our requirements are.

This chapter suggests how you can use art media to facilitate your awareness of what kind of living space best suits your needs.

137

By *life-space,* I mean not only actual environmental space but also a kind of emotional space that we sense as quite real but cannot define physically. For the sake of our discussion, I will define the two as if they were separate concepts, calling one *objective space* and the other *subjective space.* In my objective space, I look for a kind of physical space that fits my activities in interrelating with others in my environment. In my subjective space, I look for a kind of existential freedom in which I can seek my own way of being and experiencing me as I am.

In the living process, the two kinds of space overlap and intermingle; we cannot separate our emotional and our physical needs and satisfactions, nor is there any clear demarcation between our subjective and objective attitudes about space or about anything else. In experiencing our feelings about space through art media, we cannot make exact distinctions of what kind of needs we are expressing either.

Nevertheless, I will present two separate art projects through which you may be able to clarify your own feelings and ideas in a way that helps you to be more aware of your attitudes about yourself in both kinds of space.

Of course, in order to do this you must play your own game with the materials; you must endow the sheet of paper with qualities it does not, in itself, possess. It is just a sheet of paper with its own dimensions. Your prosaic mind knows that, but your imagination can transcend common sense. By using uncommon sense you can claim the ordinary paper as your territory and transform it symbolically into any kind of space you want it to be.

Let your first drawing of you in space express your sense of yourself in subjective space. While you are doing the drawing, perceiving its implications for you, and perhaps interpreting it together with other people, let yourself pretend that you exist only in relation to yourself; no other people or outside environmental forces are involved in this drawing. Of course, you know this is not possible or desirable in reality, but play the game for a while to try to discover what your personal feelings might be if there were no other elements to help or hinder you in your search for your actualized, real self.

Begin by selecting a size of paper to paint on. See this area of blank space as a symbol of what is available to use for your own self. This space represents the potentials you are capable of fulfilling; it represents your subjective feelings of the possible breadth and width of your existence. In this space, draw how you are feeling, how big, how strong, how colorful, how free, or perhaps how little, weak, pale, or restricted you perceive yourself. Your drawing on the paper describes visually the relationship of what field of inner experience is available to you and how much and in what way you are using that potential.

Simply say to yourself, "This is my space. I can use it for me in any way I want; I put me in my space with whatever imagery I find true for me." You can make your space bigger by adding more paper;

you can make it smaller by cutting or tearing; you can change the shape of your space. You can draw and paint yourself any size and shape that feels right for you. There is no wrong way; there is only your way.

While you are drawing, let go of your critical faculties, both positive and negative. Don't interpret or evaluate, just move your images in your space with whatever medium you are using. When you have finished, look at what you have done and see how you have used your space. Does your drawing say something to you? Do you know what it says? You drew a message for you. Can you read it? Is your graphic representation of you in your subjective space congruent with the reality of you in your living? Ask your own questions, and give yourself honest answers. Do some introspecting and remembering. When you have opportunities to live fully, do you respond by spreading yourself large enough to meet the challenge? Or do you shrink into your limitations to avoid any risk? Maybe you imagine yourself to be so grandiose that you never can get enough space to be you in. Maybe you see yourself as Gulliver in a terrain made for Lilliputians. Or it could be that you are so overwhelmed by the emotional space you could expand into, if you let yourself go, that you draw protective barriers to keep you securely inside circumscribed areas. Does your imagery give you any insight into how you do what you do, where you are in being who you are?

And where do you draw you on your page? In the center? In a corner? Around the sides? All over the place? What do you tell yourself? This particular experience is a subjective one in which you may or may not discover meaning for yourself.

The location people choose to be in while they work often indicates whether they prefer large amounts of free space or small, secure corners. The size of the paper an individual selects to paint on also shows a choice for large or small areas. Some personality types always choose large sheets, others always choose small sheets. I have played surreptitious games with a few of these people whose consistent choice I know from long experience; I have offered only one size of paper—medium—to the whole group. Most of the group accept my choice and work on that size, but the boldest of the wide-open spacers sometimes rebels, either by putting several sheets together or demanding, "Don't you have anything bigger to paint on? I can't do anything on this size; I need more space." On the other hand, I've watched a number of the cozy-corner types accept the medium-sized sheet without comment and then quietly fold it into a size with which they feel comfortable.

When given freedom to do so, most participants in the groups will choose sizes to suit their mood at that particular time; since their moods vary, so do the sizes of their paintings and drawings. I am one of those who prefers medium and small areas to paint on; I can cover huge sheets and I can draw on tiny cards, but ordinarily I choose fairly consistently the common size of about 20 by 30 inches. Sometimes I need to paint BIG and am frustrated if I can't do this; at other times I want a small area, 9 by 12 inches, and I feel uncomfortable when I have to fill up a larger sheet. I know for me that my preference for a certain amount of space at certain times is directly related to my variations in feelings about myself in actual living situations; sometimes events in my life are large in scope. Perhaps I am involved in a major activity, change, trauma, drama. During other phases nothing seems to happen; I am vegetating and ruminating.

Sometimes I feel physically small but my emotions, my sensing, feeling, intuiting, and thinking are big. When I stand on the edge of the Grand Canyon looking into vast distances and at mammoth forms, knowing my body's small dimensions, I am at the same time experiencing both greatness/largeness and my own smallness.

There are other times when I feel physically big, but my thoughts and emotions are small. When I am riding on a crowded bus at 5:00 p.m., standing in the aisle, my body is too big for the space I push for among the other too-big bodies; at the same time, my feelings and thinking are little and petty.

My physical dimensions remain the same, but I surely feel bigger and smaller in different situations. When I stride with long steps on a windy hill, loving life and me and things about me, alert and aware, I feel 10 feet tall. When I am weary, discouraged, and dull, I curl up in bed, feeling no larger than a small, frail child.

Sometimes I think and feel creatively; my comprehension of ideas can be so broad in range that I feel dizzy with my own breadth of vision. Sometimes I limit all my ways of perceiving; I see and feel and think on a small scale, confining myself so much into tight, narrow areas of awareness that I feel shrunken and lifeless, dead and withered.

It is hard for me to verbalize these subjective perceptions of myself as being large or small, but I can express how I feel with art materials. I can show you so that you can see: using the actual space of a sheet of paper as a symbol of the emotional space available to me, I can draw a representation—a visual metaphor—of how I am being in that space at any one time.

Some people find the whole idea of personal subjective space foreign and incomprehensible. Admittedly the concept is vague and ephemeral, since none of us can contact what I am calling subjective space directly with any of our known physical senses. Perhaps a better word would be potential or possibility. Perhaps, after all, there are no words to describe, much less explain, the inner knowing you may reach about how large or small you are in that intangible and invisible realm of what you could be.

Some people in the art groups say that illustrating their subjective space evokes sure perceptions about themselves. I ask them if they can verbalize their experience; they try and can't! I know that I increase my awareness of me when I draw me in my space, but when I try to put this insight into words, now, I feel inept and inarticulate. So I give up trying. Do the experiment and discover for yourself whether you find it meaningful.

Right now, frustrated by my own inadequacy with words, I draw myself in my space:

I've written myself into a corner!

Peller

A lovely, talented young friend of mine worked herself into feeling subjectively cornered. Peller, who has her Master's degree as an art specialist and is very competent in her profession, looks like a sexy teen-ager and often acts, for the sheer fun of it, like a silly little girl. Like a loveable fox terrier, she scampers around exploring both her subjective and objective space with a sort of enthusiastic abandon that is unnerving to some; she moves at too fast a pace for most people.

For the last three years, Peller has worked in the public school system. In many ways she liked her job and did it well, but she did not fit easily into the psychological space in which she had to work. She felt that the children were being held back from full participation in art experiences; she pushed for what she thought best; she met opposition and criticism; she felt pushed into a corner.

She began using a sketchbook diary to express her impatience with the plodding tread of some of the people around her (see Figures 34 through 38):

My silly drawings began quite spontaneously three years ago. I was attending a regular, excruciatingly boring faculty meeting at the public school where I worked as one of the elementary teachers.

I found it very difficult to listen to the mundane dialogue going on about me. I picked up a pencil. In an effort to extricate myself from the painful situation and still remain physically in the same seat with all my pent-up energy and impatience, I began my first silly drawings.

Figure 34. *"Teachers Arriving at Turtle School Each Morning."*

Figure 35. *" 'And Now I'd Like to Introduce the Superintendent of Schools to You New Teachers.' "*

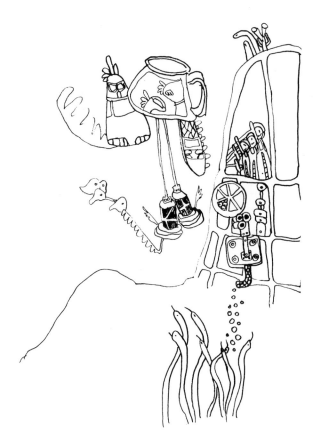

Figure 36. "Principal's Bulletin: 'Today You Should Talk to Your Class about Astronauts Landing on the Moon.'"

Figure 37. "The Kids Arrive at Bird School."

Figure 38. "Me in Bed after School, Trying to Get Back to Myself."

In my drawings I could let a little bit of myself out but still, when called on, play my expected role as a teacher in the adult world. I had to keep one ear open for fear that the teachers might catch me not listening. Subsequently, my one ear and my fantasies produced drawings that dealt with the topic of conversation. Here on paper I saw the rather absurd and frantic side of myself as a teacher in the seemingly hopeless public school situation. Here I worked out some of my rage, hostilities, and confusion by using humor.

I became addicted to this outlet and found myself taking my sketchbook to school every day and drawing during lunch with the teachers and during recess with the children.

Each drawing began on its own accord while teachers chatted around me. In my drawings I could let my own childlikeness out. The kids often peered over my shoulder at recess and soon started their own notebooks. I still do silly drawings.

Peller's art language is more subtle than her words—more sightful and caustic, too. In her drawings I see a laughing challenge to which I can respond openly: "You make us all look absurd, you and me and others. You tease and taunt and you are casually cruel; you make people angry and then you ask them to laugh with you. I welcome the release of laughter."

Since this time, Peller has done more self-exploration through art, yoga, and meditation and has become much more aware of her subjective feelings of what space is best for her. She is now in the Peace Corps in Africa near the Kalahari Desert. Her work in helping others learn how to make saleable crafts gives her plenty of space for both being and doing.

Art language is for absurdity, too—for fun, for joy! Too many people deny themselves the freedom of using art for fun; both art and words can be profound or silly, humorous or solemn, abstract or photographic, and so on. With art as with words, what our culture regards as most profound may be meaningless to you; on the other hand, something you discover for yourself either visually or verbally may not be significant for someone else. Let's try to use both ways of communicating with equal freedom.

I climb up on my soapbox and deliver evangelistic sermons to all of you readers who say plaintively, "But I can't draw a straight line without a ruler." Of course you can't, and you don't have to. Draw your own lines and don't care whether they are crooked or straight. Welcome and bless them for being naturally yours.

Draw yourself in your subjective space in any way you want; remember that the paper is the province of your inner being. Nobody can violate that space of yours unless you let him; and nobody can direct how you use it unless you want him to.

So make it your game, and do it your way. Ignore my advice if you want, and maybe you will discover and welcome some awareness uniquely your own.

SHARING SPACE

I have used *subjective space* to define our interior, personal reactions to our experiences. As these experiences change, our personal, subjective space balloons, contracts, and shifts. I use the term *objective space* to explore how we are affected by the structural physical world. Objective space is a constant in the sense that a change in our mood does not affect the physical reality of our environment: my being happy will not make an 8 by 10 foot room any larger (although subjectively, it may feel larger). Objective space is a physical characteristic that we respond to kinesthetically, each in our individual way. This means that we need to be aware of how we adapt to the physical space available to us if we are to be as in touch with ourselves as possible.

All of us—couples, families, relatives, friends, co-workers, groups of all sorts—must deal with this structuring of environmental space so that each person can have space that is privately his own and also space that is publicly shared. Needs for private and public space are likely to vary with individuals; recognizing these different needs is the first step in being able to design environments that provide maximum satisfaction for each person.

One of several ways to bring hidden conflicts and misunderstandings out is to use art media to make visible representations of interactions among the various members of the group. This is a direct way of experiencing in visual form behavioral patterns that are not easily described or perceived verbally.

The method is very simple: instead of talking about your different behaviors in the same environment, you can express them graphically by drawing together in the same space. You can use all sorts of art materials for this, but a large sheet of paper and colored chalks are the easiest. You put the paper on the floor or on a large table, and each participant chooses two colors to make his marks with. You accept the paper as your common environment; the chalk is your vehicle for depicting your individual actions in your shared space. Any number of people can get into the act, but it is usually best to begin with two. You take turns, at least in the beginning, but if your interaction gets lively, you may be drawing at the same time. No words are used until all the drawings are finished. Make as many drawings together as you feel you want to.

After you have finished these drawings and have taken a minute to allow you to return to the verbal world, discuss what the two of you experienced.

What aspects of the communal experience evoked the most intense emotional reactions? When and what did you feel when your lines were painted over? Did you establish an inviolate territory or did you build for interaction? Were you feeling on the offensive or the defensive most of the time? As you discuss, see if you can find parallels between your paper world and your actual world. In this way, you can become more aware of the demands you make on objective space— and perhaps realize what structuring you have done unconsciously and what structuring you would like to build into your life.

Recently, a training group at the Gestalt Institute in San Francisco spent a three-hour session exploring how well its members could use this project for becoming more aware of their interactions. These six people, all professionals in the fields of education and therapy, had been together in weekly group sessions for several months. They had participated in many individual art experiences, but this was the first experiment in drawing together in the same space.

I sensed that some unfinished business between participants was being covered by a very genuine desire to cooperate with each other for the common goal of becoming more perceptive in communicating with each other. Cooperation in itself is an excellent state of affairs, but when misunderstandings and possible antagonisms lie buried, the bland professed togetherness can keep people from moving into authentic contact. Feeling that some members of this group might be sitting on unhatched eggs of hostility, I suggested that they choose to draw with a partner with whom they wanted a nonverbal dialogue.

Three pairs formed quickly: Jim and Doris, Henry and Lorna, Lou and Amy.

I did not join in; I wanted to see, to listen, and to take notes. Imagine that you are sitting in a corner with me, observing how these sensible people can act out their feelings in the interest of establishing a more honest base for person-to-person relationships.

To my left are Jim and Doris. Soberly, quietly, earnestly, they take turns drawing and do not look at each other.

To my right, Henry and Lorna are intensely involved; typically, Lorna is moving her chalk with precision, filling in large solid areas, concentrating on what she is doing. Typically, Henry is moving his chalk quickly; impatient and restless, he glances around the room and turns back to Lorna to make some comment. Lorna squelches him with a frown; Henry picks up his chalk and darts lines on their drawing; Lorna erases his lines with her fist, and Henry's mouth drops open in bewilderment. Lorna placidly resumes making smooth, colorful forms on the paper between them while Henry creates sharp chalk lines in the same space with stabbing motions of his hand. Lorna and Henry stop drawing and look into each other's eyes; Henry laughs, Lorna glowers; they both return their attention to the paper; they are drawing at the same time now.

Across the room from me, Lou and Amy are using many sheets of paper. They are literally filling up space on the studio floor with ragged paper scraps and chalk dust. They are filling the room with noise, too. No words, but grunts, groans, exclamations, squeals, and shouts. Amy is ripping the paper with the vigorous strokes of her chalk; Lou jerks the torn sheet away and, laying out a clean sheet, makes some tense lines across it; Amy looks as if she is about to cry. She swoops across the new sheet with broad strokes, and they're both into the fray again.

I stay in my corner, my eyes open, receiving impressions; making no comments, I do not interfere with the real dramas being created by three pairs of people. They are engrossed in their nonverbal conversations; they seem to have forgotten my presence. For an hour, not one intelligible word is said in the studio.

Gradually, the protagonists show that they've had enough. They emerge from their experience looking a bit dazed; they glance around self-consciously, blinking their eyes as if to clear them of the impact of metaphorical imagery so they can see the physical reality of actual people in an ordinary room. I empathize with them; this shifting from one kind of reality experience to another is disorienting; it takes time to come out when you've been so far in, or to come in when you've been so far out. So we take a coffee break and then come back, sit in a circle, and begin to talk about what we have been doing.

Jim and Doris, who had worked together without obvious discord, said that they had experienced accord in creating the two drawings that they showed to us with subdued, smiling pride. The first one was mostly linear, the lines following each other all over the page in relaxed rhythm and easy spacing; in the second drawing, Jim and Doris had nonverbally communicated that they wanted to blend all the color areas together, expressing the lack of felt barriers between them. Jim and Doris were satisfied with their art creations, and their manner convinced the rest of us that they had truly depicted their comfortable personal relationship.

Henry and Lorna had no such clear communicating to report; in fact, they were still looking at each other with hostile challenges, even after the coffee break. Subsequently, though, they learned to speak more openly with each other; in the continuing group sessions, they had never accepted each other's attitude as valid. Perhaps this would have been impossible since their life styles simply didn't mesh in a mutually satisfying way. Their differences were evident in their one large drawing and later in their baffled attempts to resolve those conflicts verbally. Lorna, a self-contained competent young artist, wanted to create large, organic spaces in which she could quietly be with herself. She left plenty of space for Henry to draw in, but she expected him to stay outside her chosen territory. Henry, a volatile, action-oriented man, wanted more interplay between Lorna and himself than she would permit. Lorna had defined a smooth, green meadow that was a place for her to rest in; with red chalk, Henry had gamboled all over her muted green area, leaving messy dashes of footprints; Lorna had drawn a black boundary fence around her space; Henry had decorated it with white and yellow flowers, blurring her clear outline into grayness. With her fist and palm, Lorna then erased all of Henry's lines that touched on her smooth forms; Henry, frustrated and bewildered, started making rambling lines all around the edge of the paper. Sometimes his chalk skittered off the edges and broke. Henry was rejected and angry; Lorna was composed and adamant. They had a further private dyad over more coffee, but reported later that the best they could achieve was an agreement to disagree.

Lou and Amy related their art experience more in actions than in words; during the coffee break and while the Jim/Doris and Henry/Lorna discussions were going on, Lou and Amy had been sitting close together. Like children exhausted and relieved by a temper tantrum, they sat quietly, a bit embarrassed by their outbursts, and united by their feelings of having acted out their childishness. Actually Amy and Lou are two capable, mature women who wanted a closer friendship but who felt they needed to test each other's vitality before they could feel free to join forces in working together. Now, they co-lead a weekly art experience group; in between, they openly share their problems and joys in simultaneously being wives, mothers, and career-minded women. They grin sheepishly when they recall the spat that littered the room with chalk dust and paper scraps.

In the studio, paper and chalk are expendable and we know we are dealing with an explicit contract of direct expression and immediate feedback. We can experiment and learn from this kind of simulation game. Out in the real world, situations are more complex, and we can't isolate the parts from the whole as we can symbolically with art materials. Out in the world, we often don't even know who is drawing what lines in whose space.

For example, I visit friends who live on a short dead-end street in Berkeley. Their physical environment hasn't changed much during the last 10 years. The comfortable old houses have lost a bit of luster, the trees have grown taller, and a few more fences have been built, but essentially there's not much outward change in the neighborhood. The change is obvious, though, in the people who live there. Some of the homes are occupied by elderly people who have lived there for decades; other houses have been rented or sold to groups of students. Some students have long hair, dress in wild clothes, live communally, and are called hippies, either affectionately or derogatorily. The old-timers and the hippies share the street's common environment, but they don't share the same philosophies. So the old-timers trim their lawns and plant neat flower borders. They like to sit on their porches contemplating the clipped green of their lawns and the fresh colors of their flowers. To some of the hippies, lawns are to be lain on and flowers are to be picked; to some of the newcomers, yards are for growing organic gardens. In this single geographical environment, at least two behavioral environments co-exist, and change is inevitable in the neighborhood.

So it is with any of us who are together. Our common geography affects us all; our individual behavior affects us all; and by our behavior, both common and personal, we influence and can change our environment to some extent. But unless we choose to be hermits we must adapt to some physical and personality differences that are unchangeable. We can choose our environments to some extent and look for places and people that suit us best, but there's no way to create a living situation wherein the personalities involved can co-exist in perfect harmony and accord.

FANTASY IN SPACE

Here is an example that illustrates my thoughts about physical and psychological space. Recently I was trapped into sharing both kinds with a woman whom, with considerable malice, I shall call Mrs. P.

I was flying on a small plane that was bumping its way through the hot air currents over the mountains of Tennessee. I was taking notes on a workshop I had just attended. In my little red notebook I wrote questions to myself and lit a cigarette while I tried to answer them. Immediately the woman sitting next to me reached into her purse, pulled out a giant white handkerchief, and held it over her mouth. I hadn't noticed her before, but her white flag caught my attention immediately. With reluctant concern and in my best ladylike voice, I asked, "Does my smoking bother you?"

"Oh, no," she said. "You go right ahead and enjoy your cigarette. It's just that when anyone smokes near me, I throw up!" I put out the cigarette. She put away her handkerchief and stated triumphantly, "When Mr. P., my husband, was alive, I always made him go outside the house to smoke. When he lit up inside, I threw up!" I decided that this lady was a success! She knew how to get what she wanted. Her face showed it, too. No question wrinkles, just straight lines of hard assurance. I gave up pondering my doubts and listened to her certainties.

In a strong, flat voice she told me, "This plane doesn't sound right to me. The motor's got something wrong with it; but it doesn't matter to me if we crash. I'm saved. I've been saved since I was 7 years old when I accepted the Lord Jesus Christ as my Saviour. Are you saved?" I thought I was as saved as anyone else. "Well," she said, "there's only one way to be saved . . ."—and so on and on and on.

I laughed inwardly at our one-sided conversation. Her only recognition of me as a person was to say, "I see that you're writing in your notebook. You must be one of those career women."

I didn't have to be very astute to know from the tone of her voice and the twist of her lips that to her a "career woman" was suspect. I didn't behave normally according to her standards; she knew the right way of getting "saved." Since I was a bit vague about my chances of salvation, her missionary fervor murked the air between us as much as my cigarette smoke had earlier.

I didn't make any throwing up gestures, though, because for a while I was intrigued. She reminded me of some therapists, ministers, group leaders, and parents I've known. They, too, know the one right way to be mentally, morally, or emotionally healthy—or how to achieve whatever other rightness is necessary for salvation. Since one person's salvation may be another's damnation, the atmosphere can get fairly murky when true believers spout forth their different cure-alls.

This time I left this lady a clear field and listened, all the while making notes in my head instead of in my notebook. Mrs. P. certainly would never get involved in an art group with me or anyone else, but, I fantasized, just suppose she would, by some miracle, find herself not in her heaven but in the hell of a nonverbal session where she could not use her strident voice. Suppose we sat down with art materials rather than words between us. Suppose we tried painting together on one sheet of paper? Could we communicate?

Mrs. P. kept talking. I became bored listening, and nothing she was yakking about merited mental note-taking. So I allowed myself the luxury of going into a private fantasy, dragging Mrs. P. with me. I imagine her and me in my studio. I put a large sheet of paper on the floor, and we sit side by side in front of it. I give her a black chalk and I take some gray. "Now, Mrs. P.," I say, "Imagine that this paper is the space we are sharing on the plane—one half is mine, the other half is yours. Instead of talking, let's draw how we are using that space."

In my fantasy, she catches on fast and immediately draws:

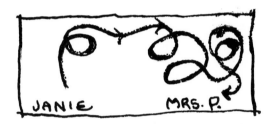

We don't use words, but I get her message: "Your cigarette smoke is violating my space."

Then I make my mark, an arrow that shows Mrs. P.'s threat to my space—her statement that she will throw up.

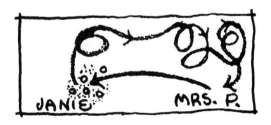

I put out my cigarette; she puts away her handkerchief. We erase the lines. We have cleared our spaces. But when Mrs. P. starts reading my notebook, she draws this to express "Your writing offends me."

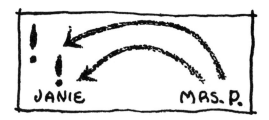

My turn. I erase her lines and draw "Keep your eyes out of my space."

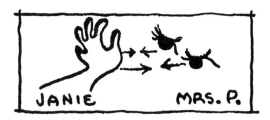

She retaliates by drawing "You need help. Let me tell you how to run your life."

I respond that I have a different view of her information: it's polluting my space as much as my smoking polluted hers earlier.

I take an extra turn to respond to her pollution: "I throw up!"

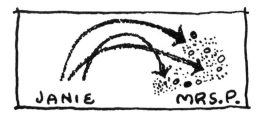

Having drowned Mrs. P. in fantasy, I felt I had finished with her in actuality. So I leaned back in my space, closed my eyes, breathed deeply, and let my mind go into nothingness.

Part Four

USING THE GESTALT ART EXPERIENCE WITH OTHERS

Chapter Nine

GESTALT ART EXPERIENCE GROUPS

ASSUMPTIONS

Living organisms, from bugs to people, are both individual and social. From the primitive bushman to the most sophisticated modern man, grouping is a common phenomenon. People naturally form groups because groups fill individual, social, environmental, and cultural needs. The purpose, the members, the values, and the goals vary from time to time and from place to place. Today, our groups include sensitivity, encounter, and growth groups because we seek to interact with new individuals as well as to broaden our group experience to extra-familial and extra-vocational encounters.

This chapter will deal with the format and the rationale of the groups I lead. By applying gestalt psychology and gestalt therapy to what I call the gestalt art experience, I emphasize the holistic view of any person's growth into physical, mental, and emotional health.

I work mostly in groups with people who are actively and con-structively taking responsibility for realizing their own potential. What we call our goals—whether self-actualization, development of personal identity, or finding our true self—isn't as important as our attitude toward each other. Of course, the individuals in the program vary greatly in their capacity for self-direction, and all of them have periods of frustration. Our agreement is that we will be available to each other but that each individual can and must find for himself what will best ful-fill his own felt needs.

I assume that each participant is in the process of becoming who he really is; I support anything that contributes to his sense of responsibility and self-worth. As much as is reasonable, I focus on what is vital in each personality and avoid labeling individual behavior and attitudes. I do not push for adjustment to any so-called normal standards but encourage each person to expand his awareness of how he perceives himself, to accept himself as he is, to find his own way of being, and to trust his own sense of what will lead him toward integration and autonomy.

We work in small groups of about 10 people, the leaders participating along with other members. The art work—done individually, in pairs, or as a group—is used as a bridge for communicating between the inner experience of each person and his verbalization about it with others. I discourage analyzing, explaining, or even interpreting the images and encourage describing the figures in terms of the perceptual awareness of self-discovery in creating the forms.

Though we primarily use graphic art materials, we add other media to facilitate experience, exploration, and expression. We make noises as we work. We move from one environment to another and sometimes build life-size structures in the studio, outside in the park, in the country, or on the beach. In these we recognize and respond to feelings about space, distance, closeness, and touching. We explore tactile and sensory reactions with a wide range of man-made structures, natural forms, and other human bodies. We dance our feeling states with or without music. We create fantasies and dramas and act various self-selected roles, sometimes using self-designed masks to display our various personas. We activate as much of ourselves as we are able to at any time.

I assume that all people are to some extent naturally creative; that they can rediscover their creativity in experiencing their wholeness; that this experience is enriching for almost anyone; that some people find the gestalt art experience to be effective in developing their own sense of balance and centeredness.

Accepting a definition of *gestalt* as "the visual perception of single, completed configurations, where the whole appears to dominate the parts,"[1] and adding the concept that "vision, in daily life as well as in art, functions as a part of the total mind,"[2] I assume that the felt needs of any person incline him toward selective perception, not only in what he perceives but also in how he acts. Since working with art materials is a way of acting, I carry this concept farther and assume that any person (if he feels free to do so) will create with art materials a symbol

[1] L. L. Whyte, ed., *Aspects of Form* (London: Percy Lund Humphries, 1951), p. 5.

[2] *Ibid.,* p. 203.

(representation, substitute) for whatever is most important to him at any time (the figure in the background of his total life at present).

Furthermore, I find that most people in my groups, in the act of creating forms, recognize and realize for themselves some thoughts and feelings that they were not consciously aware of previously. In other words, the experience of creating concrete forms makes real and brings into cognition some feeling/thinking states that the person was only vaguely aware of before. Many people can then see that the patterns of their art forms symbolize how they pattern their attitudes and behavior in living: thus, seeing a clear gestalt in their artwork can lead to perceiving a clear gestalt of themselves as personalities. This holistic recognition of themselves can lead to an increased acceptance of individual autonomy and responsibility.

My experience is that this kind of self-discovery art can and often does lead not only to self-realization, but also to an increased capacity for communication, understanding, relatedness, and commitment with others.

When you come to a gestalt art experience group you are curious. Are we going to do therapy? Are we going to create art forms? Are we going to have fun? Are we going to play games? Are we going to be childish? Are we going to act like idiots? Yes, we are going to do all of these things.

We are a group of people who have come here to experience together. We are reasonably mature and well-adjusted, and we can function together. Well-educated and knowledgeable about ourselves and our world, we talk, listen, read, and know that we are living in a time of cultural change. We are involved in the changes going on around us and within us. Obviously we are willing to explore new ways of learning and living that might help us to know what we want to be. So, among the many other things we do, we participate in an art experience group.

I am a participant in the group as well as its leader. I provide space to work in, materials to work with, and suggestions as to how we might work together.

You may not have used art materials since you were in kindergarten; you may say that you cannot draw or paint. I tell you that you can. When you take a piece of colored chalk or a paint-loaded brush in your hand and move it around on a sheet of paper, you are making a drawing or a painting. When you take a blob of clay and shape it with your hand movements, you are making a piece of sculpture. Its aesthetic value is irrelevant. What is relevant is that you express yourself in creating a form.

Some of you may have previous training and experience in art. Unless you are a copyist, your art form inevitably expresses something of you, but if you use skill instead of spontaneity, your expression will show your competence more than your awareness.

I ask you to put aside, for now, any consideration of yourself as an artist and simply to use the art media as vehicles of expression. While you are here, I ask you to accept some dos and don'ts that I find necessary for getting the most out of this kind of experience. I find that the same rules of the game help me in living, too. Perhaps they will help you see and be more yourself both while you are here and when you are somewhere else.

I begin each group session with basic don'ts: While we are together, don't hope for anything to happen. Don't expect anything to happen. Don't try to solve problems. Don't look for problems to solve. Don't figure out what you are doing. Don't analyze what you are doing. Say to yourself that we think too much already. We are naturally whole—mind, body, and soul are one—yet we keep trying to separate these parts, exhausting ourselves in the futile task of separating that which is inseparable.

Most of us use our thinking capacity as a tool for cutting ourselves into pieces. We compute ourselves into robots; we intellectualize ourselves into rigidity. We forget that our well-developed brains are only a part of our total organism. As a whole, you and I are each a gestalt, a process, a pattern intricately and awesomely interwoven. We each have infinite possibilities for awareness, growth, and excitement. We limit our possibilities in many ways, primarily with our thinking.

In the art experience group, do let your brain rest and relax. Do give yourself permission to let happen what will. Do allow yourself to be quiet. Do listen to yourself and others. Do receive messages without judging them. Do trust the awareness you receive through your senses.

These dos and don'ts seem so simple, and they are. You may say, "Any child can do that," and you are right. Any healthy, young child does whatever he is doing with all of himself. When he is building a sand castle, he creates a form with his movements, feeling the damp sand, knowing that he is building his sand castle the way he wants, and for no reason at all except that right now he feels good making a sand castle.

I remember how I felt as a child—simply and beautifully aware of me and the sand and the air about me and of my creation. I was whole within myself and freely one with my environment. You may remember being like that, too.

As adults, we have lost, or at least misplaced, the single-minded concentration of being totally in the moment. We think about one thing while we are doing another. Although we know many facts and figures about ourselves, we have very little self-awareness. We are searching for some way to find that missing something.

You may come to a gestalt group to figure out what gestalt therapy is about. You have questions and goals, and you want solutions. You may be trying to function like a computer, taking in data, processing it, and coming out with answers. You are not a computer, though, and when you try to act like one, you defeat yourself as a human being.

The "thinking-machine man" acts like a computer with its wires crossed. Lights flash, tapes come out by the yard, and holes are punched. With this dramatic display and brilliance come lots of answers, all of them seemingly fraught with philosophical truth, but they don't make sense. The super-intellectual who knows it all, who has quick, parrying answers, who habitually pushes buttons (his own and others) is no more able to be a whole human being than the computer is. He gloats about his ability to produce complex configurations of thinking patterns, tangles himself in his figurings, and gets his mind into intricacies of thought that are closed circuits. He makes circles and knots with whys and becauses.

The intellectual becomes an idiot. When his verbal formulations are recognized as meaningless, he becomes aware of his helplessness to know or express anything and hasn't any way of getting in touch with the reality of himself. If this person knows that he's in limbo and can accept being where he is (that he has lost his mind), he can come to his *senses* by the simple process of getting in touch with them and using them.

The art experience is one way to contact yourself through your senses. Dancing, drumming, working with clay, drawing, and painting—without trying to figure out why you are doing what you are doing—can help you know yourself on a sensory level. Without trying, you make sense.

When you can "get out of your head" for a while, you gladly and guilelessly enter into creative fantasies that are non-rational and yet that make sense. Using art materials, you can become so involved in what you are *doing* that your whole body expresses a relaxed concentration. You are "playing," as healthy children do when there is no separation between work and play or between seriousness and joy. Watching your movements and your faces, I see expressions of delight, wonder, anger, sadness, and gaiety coming and going without apparent conscious effort. I see you composing silently the music of your own inner rhythm, using your whole self and your art materials as instruments, improvising spontaneously and confidently without striving or groping. You flow with your own music, and I watch you without any sense that I am intruding. You are freely with yourself. You are being yourself.

OUTPATIENTS ET AL.

With the title, "Training Consultant in the Use of Art Therapy," I conducted a two-day workshop in the day-care center of a large mental health hospital. I led both experiential and didactic sessions and participated in discussion groups with occupational and recreational therapists on the hospital staff.

One morning we had an art experience group that included outpatients, therapists, and two chaplains. I didn't know who was who and insisted that everyone participate—no observers allowed! So, 20 of us sat in a circle on the floor, each with a lump of damp clay. My directions were simple:

"Pick up the lump of clay in front of you and find out how you can make it into different shapes. Change the shape as often as you want. Make one shape that shows something you don't like about yourself and another shape to show something you do like about you. After we have finished, you may talk about what you have made, or you may keep the clay and not talk about it at all."

Almost everyone begins, but a few just hold the clay and stare blankly. As I model my clay, I watch the others. Across the room, three overweight, middle-aged women sit close together, obviously uncomfortable on the floor. Their faces are expressionless, and I see no evidence that they are communicating. At one moment all three, like automatons, get up and sit in three chairs, still holding their clay in lax hands. Their faces remain vacant. I see no sign of emotion—no interest or resistance, just passive resignation.

Then one of the women begins squeezing the clay and glancing at it furtively. After a while she puts both of her hands into the act and moves them animatedly, though she still mostly looks out into space as if she's not aware what her hands are doing. Finally she looks down at her clay, and suddenly her face is transformed by a glad, mischievous smile. She looks straight into my eyes and grins widely, as if she is sharing a joke with me. I return a smile to her, thanking her for showing her pleasure to me. During the rest of the session she holds her one small image in her two hands, turning it around and looking at it quizzically. Sometimes a transient smile lights up her face, and sometimes she is pensive.

When we have finished making the images and I invite people to speak if they want to, she says in a rush, "I don't want to talk about what I've made and I don't want to show it to anybody, but I found out something about me and I want to take this home with me to remind me." I say that she may and add, "I like the way you smile." She replies firmly, "Thank you. I feel good smiling right now. It's been a long time since I've felt good enough to smile." I cannot see her clay figure clearly because she keeps it cradled in her hands. She does not speak throughout the remainder of the session, but her face reflects interest in whatever anyone else is doing and saying. Somehow, in making her figure, she not only got in touch with something dormant in herself, she also became actively interested in other people.

A few other participants talk, some hesitantly and some with confidence. The rest of us listen to an involved interchange between two men who are sitting facing each other across the circle. I observe during this dialogue and say nothing; obviously this is a personal confrontation. Both of the men are slight in build, and, as I look from one to the other, I am aware how much they resemble each other. Their imagery in clay is similar, too. They have each made figures of two connected round balls, something like the dumbbells used for weight lifting. One man, Howard, has placed his construction in an upright position so that one ball is over the other; Phil, the other man, has his figure lying horizontally, and the connecting bar is thinner.

Howard speaks first with a measured, somewhat flat tone, "This is me—two parts of me. I like me when I am being the bottom ball; here I am on the ground, just being a human being with other human beings. I feel comfortable here and real." Howard's hand half-encircles the lower form as he perfects its solid roundness. He moves his hand up the cylindrical column rather gingerly and touches the upper globe with his fingertips as he continues speaking. "But sometimes I put myself up on a pedestal, and when I'm up here I feel uneasy; I preach at people as if they are all below me. When I'm up so high I talk down to people—that makes me feel superior. But when I realize that I can't come down from my tower, that I have trapped myself into staying up above everybody else, then I feel lonely and frightened. I am ashamed to admit that I don't know how to unlock my own trapdoor, and I'm too proud to ask for help, so I pretend I like being up on top. That's the part of me I don't like—the me that is alone and afraid; especially I don't like my hypocrisy when I deny my loneliness. . . . I really don't know. . . ."

Howard's voice retreats into a drifting, sad monologue. He's looking at his image solemnly and is startled when Phil begins speaking with staccato stridency—impatiently, angrily. "Look, Doc, your thing looks like mine, except that you're standing up and I'm lying down. I'm about giving up; nobody likes me; nobody understands—don't understand myself. I got two parts—these two balls—don't know which is which—they're two parts of me, though. I want to get them together but when I push them together, they both smash, and when I pull them apart, I get all torn up. Sometimes I feel like I'm getting better, but most of the time I just feel like I'm not ever going to get better. People keep telling me to pull myself together, but they don't tell me how! Right now, I feel like I'm tearing this whole thing to pieces—like I'm being torn to pieces!" Phil pulls the balls apart and holding one in each hand, he glares at Howard with glittering eyes. I am tense and anxious, wondering if Phil will precipitate a crisis situation in this group. Howard, who had seemed so remote a few moments before, meets Phil's intense stare directly, and neither his eyes nor his voice wavers as he answers,

"Maybe you're right, Phil. Perhaps we are more alike than I've been admitting. I'd like to talk with you later, when we have more time. You bring your figure and I'll bring mine, and we'll try finding out what we have in common."

Phil holds his rigid pose for another second and then relaxes. He joins together the battered lumps of clay, looks at them and then back to Howard. He sighs, "Okay, Doc. Maybe that would help." The room is silent. Phil seems oblivious to anyone else as he pats, pushes, and shapes his clay; he turns his head from side to side, looking at the figure from different angles. Minutes tick by and still we are silent. Phil comes out of his trance-like self-involvement with startling suddenness; his darting eyes, taut muscles, and clenched fists indicate his readiness for battle. As he senses the supportive attitude of many group members, he smiles sheepishly and then proudly; leaning back, he seems relieved and spent. My own anxiety subsiding, I look around into the faces of the others in the room. Am I only imagining that some of the participants are sending the message, "My hero!" in Phil's direction?

The session over, the patients file out for lunch in the colorful cafeteria. A few say something pleasant to me; most of them say nothing; Phil flashes a brilliant smile and scuttles out the door with his clay image clutched closely.

Some of the staff leave the room without saying anything to me. Others gather around me, discussing the experience. Howard, whom I now know is a psychiatrist, thanks me with a dignified, "This has been a most rewarding experience for me," and goes his way with the clay held rather carefully away from the tailored business coat he's put on. There are smears of clay on his pants, though.

I am disquieted and feeling shaky after the intensity of the group art session so I use lunch time to be alone and evaluate as much as I can what happened during the morning before I begin the afternoon's scheduled discussion group. I don't know who will attend or what their attitude will be, but I assume that they will ask me questions about my particular approach and use of gestalt art experience. If I am to answer their inquiries with some clarity, I must be able to answer at least some of my own with honesty. This kind of intrapersonal searching for answers has become habitual to me; like an old dog chewing on a big bone, I gnaw away hoping to taste the marrow. About today's session, I feel both uneasy and excited. I do not know either the staff or the patients in this setting, so I find it difficult to interpret their responses; however, the director of the training program is interested enough in what I am doing to invite me and pay me well for these two days, so I feel some self-confidence. I had been adamant with those dignitaries who wanted to "just observe." They had looked surprised when I suggested they take off their coats, roll up their sleeves, sit on the floor, and get their hands into a lump of clay—but they had done so, and at least some of them showed enthusiasm.

I know from many experiences how potent modeling personal imagery in clay can be in evoking repressed emotions, and yet I had led the group in that direction, knowing that some of the patients might become agitated—some of the staff, too! The interchange between Phil and Howard in the presence of patients and colleagues—how had that affected Howard's professional image? He had said that the experience was rewarding for him; was it also damaging? Was he now regretting that he had ever participated in the group? I could imagine him sitting in his office somewhere in the hospital complex, cleaning the clay from under his fingernails, muttering, "How did I get involved in coming out so openly with my personal feelings? Would it be better if I kept myself on a pedestal when I'm with patients?" On the other hand, I can also fantasize Howard and Phil being together, using their symbolic structures constructively toward building better communication.

So I play the mental game of "on the one hand and on the other hand"; my left hand is a part of me that is the true believer in gestalt art experience and all that implies for me; my right hand is a part of me that is the skeptic who doubts and criticizes my brashness.

True believer: This way of using art materials is a direct method of experiencing that breaks through intellectual barriers and gets patients and therapists into immediate contact on a primary level.

Skeptic: This way is foolish and irrelevant to psychotherapy. The patient is seriously disturbed. The therapist must use his skill for curing the sickness of the patient, not for expressing his own personal needs and desires.

True believer: The patient needs to be contacted on a person-to-person basis. This kind of art experience is one way of eliciting personal contact that is productive for both patient and therapist.

Skeptic: Your approach is nonsense and is destructive in the therapist-patient interaction.

True believer: That's your belief. This is my belief. Others work according to their beliefs. I can speak only for myself.

At this point I realize that I am trying to resolve, all by myself in one lunch hour, an issue that many psychologists, therapists, and educators are debating in thousands of words and hours. I remind myself that this particular mental hospital set up as a research center represents an honest effort on the part of responsible people to find out what approaches work best with what patients. The doctors, psychologists, therapists, social workers, and ministers represent many philosophies and schools of thought. They, too, are questioning with skepticism their own beliefs and those of others with whom they work. But each is work-

ing according to his own beliefs, just as I am doing; all of us are considering many questions and finding some answers as we go along.
I know that the questions I ask myself cannot be answered simply; they are too far-reaching for my hands to grasp all at once. So my true-believer part and my skeptic part agree to a truce for now. My hands fold together, and I snooze briefly.

The afternoon session was devoted entirely to discussing the many questions that come up daily in this mental hospital as well as in others. A practitioner—whether psychotherapist, medical doctor, adjunctive therapist, religious advisor, or attendant—is a unique individual with his own professional viewpoint, life-style, and personality. The practitioners' one commonality is that they work in the same setting, caring for the best interests of the patients. Aside from the many difficulties inherent in treating mental illness itself, staff members of a large institution have the additional problem of agreeing among themselves on what therapeutic treatments are best for their patients.

The people in the group this afternoon can be roughly classified as adjunctive therapists; of the dozen persons sitting around a long table in a conference room, I know that two are called recreational therapists, one young woman leads encounter groups for teen-agers, and an older woman uses body and dance movement therapeutically. Their spheres of activity overlap considerably, and they coordinate their work as much as possible. They admit that they don't have perfect teamwork among themselves, but they all agree on wanting more cooperation and collaboration "from up there"—from the doctors and psychotherapists.

In their own building, the adjunctive therapists have facilities and materials for all sorts of artwork. They are interested in how they can best use what they have available. The outpatients come for regular groups. As with the group this morning, the patients are mostly apathetic and have to be encouraged to take initiative for any self-directed action. Is it wiser to let them come out of their state of indifference of their own accord or to push them into art activity? What kind of art? Making copies from molds? Crafts projects? Free painting? How about the way I use art materials as a tool for getting people in touch with themselves and others? Is that a dangerous approach to use with people who are barely making their way in the world? Is it better for all concerned that they remain inactive, emotionally at least?

Each of us humans is both strong and fragile. Although human contact can be strengthening and enriching, I realize that pathology can be a structure built to avoid contact, both with others and with oneself. To tamper with a need great enough to create such a pathology is to tamper with powerful responses, and I'm not comfortable "tampering." I prefer the individual to be able to take responsibility for his own responses: that's why I work with people who can take this responsibility. Perhaps my best addition here, where the patients can't do so, is to help the hospital staff become more responsibly response-able. Then they can become more sensitive to the possibilities of slowly evoking real contact when their patients are capable of it.

I'm idealistic enough to believe that each person strives to become more response-able. I'm realistic enough to know that this is a slow, painful process that may be best supervised by those who have a long-term, responsible relationship with the patient and who know pathology through long study.

So I finish my two-day stay with good feelings and many thoughts. I have presented my approach and way of working; I have seen how others approach the same general goal from different viewpoints and with various methodologies. I wish us all well.

ON-GOING GROUP

For a dozen people in San Francisco, Monday night was art group night; for almost a year we were together from eight in the evening until around midnight. In between the Monday nights we saw, talked, and worked with each other in various combinations and activities; sometimes on the weekend we had all-day extracurricular sessions just because we wanted to. We were one unit in the on-going training group in the Gestalt Institute of San Francisco. My co-leader, clinical psychologist Abe Levitsky, and I presented learning experiences and evaluated what was going on with different individuals and in the group as a whole. We realized that this group was not a passive entity to be directed into any preconceived model of what a training group should be. These 10 people were contributing their distinct color and form to the ever-varying pattern of our Monday-night adventure.

Though Abe and I designed the evening's activities around some particular concept or aspect of gestalt and art therapy, we never knew until it happened, what we—all of us—might be getting into. The group members deferred to us as leaders just so far and no farther. If any of them felt that either of us was not coming up to his standards, he let us know about it and deference went out of the picture. I liked that. I liked us; I liked our serious searching, our bafflement, our trust, support, humor, disagreements; I liked our honesty.

Especially I liked our doing artwork together, exploring and discovering ways to use art both therapeutically and as a medium for communication. And we did communicate: graphically, physically, and verbally, we were an articulate crew. Amela was from Israel; in her rich contralto voice she used American hip phrases and Yiddish words all mixed together to describe her paintings and experiences. Norman, a bearded 50-year-old art therapist, spoke a sonorous basso profundo when interpreting his perceptions. Roz's words wove a network of fantasies like the interwoven lines of her drawings. Ted didn't say much in words, but when he did, he was to the point. Margie looked like Alice in Wonderland when her hair fell past her shoulders and like a debutante when it was piled high on her head; only her clinical approach indicated that she was also a psychologist. Hal was working on his Ph.D., doing research in visual perception; he sometimes apologized for his intellectualizations with a diffident grin. Cory was a painter and a conscientious objector doing his alternative service teaching art to retarded children. Gilda taught art, painted, and led groups in art awareness; she was young, exotic, and laughed about her Brooklyn background. Celia was from Virginia, and her years of working in the ghetto had made her lovely smile a bit rueful at times but hadn't squelched her enthusiasm for making living a more beautiful experience. Neil was a high school principal, somewhat disillusioned by his 20 years with the educational system, but still looking for innovative ways of teaching.

So Monday night was a time for a dozen people who were already knowledgeable and experienced to add to their repertoire of knowing and experiencing.

One evening we did some frank "regression in the service of the ego." In fantasy we went back into our childhood memories to a time when each of us was living through a bewildering phase. We assumed the child-role and acted with each other as we would have done had we been friends then. We were all being 6 to 10 years old; we talked to each other of our likes, dislikes, fears, hopes, frustrations, and problems. We teased, sympathized, fought, and made up; we were forlorn, domineering, fearful, boastful. Bad and good, we relived what we remembered.

Then we painted like the children we had been, with messy fingerpaints in disarray on the studio floor. We let our colorful papers dry while we cleaned up, drank coffee, and, as discriminating adults, discussed the experience and interpreted the paintings.

"I felt like crying when I did that painting. I was such a shy little girl—so sad and afraid to use bright colors. I still choose black a lot and feel guilty if I use too much orange and pink."

"My painting looks now as if I put a grid of bars all over it— I didn't realize I was doing it, but that's the way I felt when I was ten— trapped. That's my biggest problem now—being afraid I can't be free."

"Whatever my painting is, it sure looks sexy. I used to worry about my sexiness—in fact, I do now."

"What I put on the paper doesn't show what I felt very well. Those smears are supposed to be eyes of the priests and nuns who were always looking at me. That's when I learned to lie. I confessed to sins I hadn't done at all so they'd stop accusing me. Now I accuse myself when I'm not guilty!"

Much talk—interpreting our own paintings, projecting onto those of others, some further acting out of the child who is yet within us

sophisticated adults—and it was midnight. We each had grown-up
responsibilities for tomorrow, so we reluctantly left unfinished business
for next Monday's session.

There's always unfinished business; there always will be.
I mulled this over as I was lying in bed listening to the night sounds of
the city streets: the thrum of tires on damp asphalt, the sliding screech
of brakes, the wail of a siren, the heartbeat rhythm of rock music, the
couple arguing next door, the homosexuals across the backyard having
a party, the people upstairs having a party.

I received these sounds and sights passively, detached and
with no sense of involvement. I did not know the people who were my
neighbors, and they did not know me. None of us took the time to do
more than nod polite recognition as we passed each other on stairs and
sidewalks. So that night, as on many other nights, I am with them only
in environmental space. Our lives do not touch. I wonder how many of
them know only the sadness and alienation of big-city living. I don't feel
sad or alienated. I hope that my neighbors' lives include a sense of belonging. I have brought home with me a sense of belonging with the
people in the art group. We do know each other; we do take time in the
sessions and between them for person-to-person confrontation and
understanding. We do not limit our relationship to the minimal requirements for professional working together. We want more from each
other; we feel that the added dimension of genuine contact and communication is the most essential part of our professional work. All of
our training in techniques, structures, and methodology is meaningless sham unless we evoke and develop the reality of knowing and being
known. For me, that's what counts most in any learning process. The art
materials and the words are vehicles for getting to know ourselves
and each other as we are; for seeing our similarities and differences;
for accepting our individualities; for being available to each other to
whatever extent that's possible.

As I think of how we support each other in the art group, I also
recognize that it is impossible for us to take care of all the unfinished
business of our needs. As a group we are in process, and always there
are changing relationships and discoveries of differing patterns among
us. We are there for each other through these changes; we choose to be
together because we share some common values and commitments.
Suddenly I realized that my feelings about the people whose sounds
were reaching me had changed; I realized that the music, the hilarity of
the party, the arguments, and even the siren were telling of other group
activities. Out there in the night city, people were choosing to be together for their own reasons; their life-styles might be different from
those we shared in the art group, but they too were in process with each
other. Those strangers to me were also person to person in their living;
they, too, belonged in some group.

So what happens in a group? Very complex and very simple.

The same things happen that happen in any human living situation. We come together for some kind of activity, and we have a choice: we can act our accustomed roles and leave the group without giving or taking anything much, or we can take the chance of being open to new ways of experiencing and in the give-and-take find something of immense value to ourselves. That's what I think we're doing in the art group— offering and accepting invaluable perceptions, which we both keep and pass on to others. I feel glad.

SUGGESTIONS TO
GROUP LEADERS

People have always formed groups to do things together that they cannot or do not want to do alone. Whether it is funerals or dances, prayer meetings or hell raisings, individuals naturally gravitate to like-minded others to share some experiences.

For some years now in our culture, a phenomenon called a *group movement* has been steadily growing and receiving wide publicity. Some like the idea and join in. Others deride it as cultist and unnatural—maybe even as threatening and with sinister motives for undermining traditional, conservative views of the American as a self-made, individualistic person who can make his own way without needing support, approval, or inspiration from strangers.

In spite of much publicity that presents organized groups as strange and threatening, many sane, sensible people join in planned groups without regarding themselves or the things they do as bizarre or as being significantly different from their usual activities.

Some of these groups come about as a natural consequence of people who know each other personally and who choose to arrange regular meetings for further communication and seeking in an area of interest they already share. Other groups are organized by persons who feel they have a particular ideology they would like to share with others. Some groups are designed to fit needs our society exhibits; the designers believe they can help in filling those needs.

Some intentionally created group situations are organized and advertised with the more or less frankly stated aim of cashing in on many persons' inability to provide in their ordinary living situation any kind of extraordinary activity exciting enough to get them out of their state of chronic boredom.

The most expansive and inclusive kinds of groups can be very loosely called *personal growth groups.* Many of these are formed in existing institutions—religious organizations, schools, social service centers, mental health communities, hospitals, and even in industrial and business corporations. During the past few years, growth centers have been established all over this country and in Europe; these centers are consistently optimistic that they can and do answer a genuine need in our culture. Thousands of mature, functioning people attend growth groups voluntarily; I assume that this shows recognition of a need in our society and a movement toward filling that need. Beyond that, I am quietly excited by the possibilities of how much the people who choose to seek personal growth for themselves and others can spread a belief and put into action alternative solutions to some of our social problems. Perhaps they can even add creative vision and applications that go beyond the doleful attitude of "we can't even solve our present problems" to the daring assumption of "we can outgrow at least some of our problems if we have the courage to put our energies together to stretch our psychic dimensions."

I consider gestalt art experience groups as being part of a broad cultural evolution that is growing due to many people's recognition that we can all benefit if we voluntarily explore new ways of perceiving our potential and at the same time take individual responsibility for using our capacities in whatever activity we feel most capable and effective.

My suggestions to group leaders, then, are based on my individual perception of what I consider good and valuable outgrowths of group activity.

Throughout this book, I have used the word *leader* to refer to my role in these groups. I don't really like that word and don't think it truly states my relationship to the group. But I can't think of a better word. The words *facilitator, teacher, trainer, therapist, consultant,* and so on are used by me and by others, but none of them satisfy me, either. I prefer not to use a noun title at all but rather to use a verb form such as: sometimes I am leading, sometimes teaching and/or facilitating, training, modeling, offering therapy, consulting, advising, participating, and a lot of the time I am simply experiencing and learning along with everybody else. Since those of us who are responsible for programming and directing group activities must tag ourselves with some sort of label, I will call us *leaders* and not bother too much about the connotations.

Most important, I think, you who lead groups are responsible for being aware of yourself enough so that you can feel and behave in the group with honesty and openness. I suggest that you share with the group, whenever it seems appropriate, whatever tensions, doubts, boredoms, anxieties, pleasures, and other feelings you may be experiencing. In other words, I suggest you be yourself, not only for your own sake but also to assure others that they do not have to play phony roles in order to find acceptance.

I think you can realize your potential as a guide only if you pay attention to your own preferences for the kinds of people you like to be with, the kind of approach that is most natural to you, and the physical-psychological environment that is most compatible with your temperament. Finding out with whom and in which circumstances you are at your best may take time and some trial-and-error experiences, but I feel strongly that anyone who takes the responsibility of facilitating the personal growth of others must not avoid the old dictums of "Know thyself" and "To thine own self be true." My own hardest work is to face, accept, and be honest with myself—a sort of inner housecleaning that I feel I must do when I sense I am too cluttered up inside to have any space for receiving any other person's messages.

As much as you possibly can, create a physical environment for the group you lead in which you feel most right. All people are affected by what is and is not in the space around them; many people are not aware of this effect on a conscious level but they respond on an emotional level. My own preference is for a space that feels comfortably open to inside and outside; that has a large, open space so the group can sit in a circle, and a smallish nook that a person can crawl into, at least temporarily, when he literally wants to withdraw from the circle. I prefer that people sit and work on the floor, so I provide pillows with washable covers and have a floor that can become a big drawing board and can be scrubbed clean. I have some chairs around for those who really can't floor-sit and some movable tables. Mostly, though, I find that tables and chairs not only evoke schoolchild intimidations, but also they get between people and keep them at a distance from each other.

I suggest that you try to provide lighting that can be bright enough for people to work by but that can be dimmed when the mood is for quiet meditative conversation or silence. Dimmer switches are not expensive and are easily installed.

A record player and a variety of mood-music records are useful between sessions. I rarely use music while people are doing art because I want them to find their own inner rhythm and not follow one imposed on them by an outside source.

At least one wall should be free for people to pin up drawings as they want. I don't keep paintings, especially those done by master artists, on the walls; I don't want people even subliminally to get the idea that they are supposed to produce masterpieces.

Naturally, I create in my studio the atmosphere that I like best. You may have entirely different ideas, but I suggest that part of your responsibility is to be at least aware of the space you are asking people to grow in and, like a good gardener, to do what you can to provide the most favorable conditions for healthy and productive maturation.

In art experience groups, the art materials themselves are one of the richest sources of nourishment for those who have planted themselves in your garden soil. So don't stint on materials; they need not be expensive or of professional quality, but there should be variety and quantity. And, very important to me, these materials should be placed so they can be seen and easily obtained by group members. I want the participants to feel that those materials belong to them, that each person is free to choose and use whatever he senses will best serve his expressive, experiential needs. At the beginning of workshops I ask people to explore the shelves, boxes, and baskets so they will be familiar with what is around and so feel more at home.

While people are doing artwork, they sometimes get so excited that they spill paint, tear paper, and splatter the other fellow's paintings; sometimes the studio seems entirely chaotic! But the delightfully amazing thing I've found out is that when people feel they are responsible for choosing how much of the materials to use and how messy they can be, they usually also feel responsible for cleaning up and restoring some kind of order.

I believe that this alternating rhythm of creating chaos and restoring order is natural and should not only be accepted but actively sought and supported in the group experience. The rhythmic sequence of contrasting emotional states and acting out should be recognized, encouraged, and used constructively.

One of the most basic human rhythms is that of moving from making active contact with the public world outside you and then withdrawing into an introspective private world inside you. In the enculturation process, most of us have been taught that withdrawal into one's self is anti-social—that it means rejecting the real world and implies neurotic self-absorption. In gestalt-oriented groups, the rhythm of contact and withdrawal is not considered negative but positive, each person finding his natural rhythm and flowing with it.

I suggest activities that draw people into contact with each other and then require them to withdraw from others to get in touch with their private selves. For instance, if you observe that the group members seem to be so totally withdrawn from each other that no contact is being made, you can propose a group painting in which all participants paint on a large sheet, discovering how or if they can find a way to co-exist, symbolically, in such close and limited proximity to others. Don't make rules that push for cohesiveness, antagonism, support, opposition, or any other prescribed way of relating: allow the participants to discover for themselves, each in his own way, the kind of contact they make. When the group painting is finished, ask each person to find a space to be alone in and paint his private feelings about the group experience. This gives each person time, space, and energy to pay attention to his inner experiences and perhaps to assimilate and integrate the unrecognized but often polarized feelings of need for both contact and withdrawal. Encourage people to consider what timing or rhythm is best for them; encourage them to respect their own perceptions.

Finally, I suggest that you, as leader, realize and make explicit to others that any group gathering, whether brief or extended, is a reality experience. Try to support the idea that this special time can be related to each person's situation when he returns to his daily living.

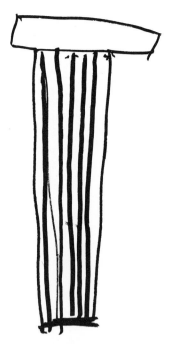

"You are a pillar of strength, calm and implacable."

"You are not too solid, but the holes are space for growing. You're reaching in many directions."

"You are forceful, gentle, cold, and funny."

"You are a deeply sensitive human whose exterior suggests a kind of Jupiter-like certainty. But you reveal inner turbulence."

Figure 39. Four members of a group say "I See You" about the co-leader of their group.

Most of the people who come to arranged groups are strangers to each other when they arrive, so early in the workshop I propose that each participant make a quick portrait of every other person and exchange signed portraits with everyone else. The portraits can be and usually are simple symbolic impressions, but in making them each member must see the other person as a presence and must concretely delineate some perception of that person. In the exchange of portrait-impressions, I ask that the two people involved move toward each other and make a few simple, direct statements to each other. Thus it is impossible for anyone to ignore anyone else completely. This exercise is usually relaxed and light with a lot of amusement at everyone's feeling of inadequacy to do 10 portraits in 30 minutes and openly expressed, common self-consciousness. When this activity is finished, I suggest that each person take his portraits home with him as a reminder of these people who are with him in the here-and-now of the group experience. They always value these portraits, and they are frequently used as referents in interchanges during later sessions.

Another crucial time when I think it important that people recognize living reality is when the group experience nears its close. Each person is about to leave a special situation in which he has almost certainly experienced some new awarenesses, some new relationships; often, they have let down defenses they customarily use in the outside world. Now they must return to their families, their friends, their jobs— maybe they must return to loneliness, to isolation, to difficult predicaments. Perhaps they return gladly to share their new perceptions with someone. But in any case, they are leaving one kind of environment and going to another, so I want them to take with them something of their own that at least symbolizes a bridge for possibly enriching and vitalizing their day-to-day lives.

Near the end of the workshops I ask people to create some self-perception image and speak, if they want, of how they feel about leaving this experience and going into another, about the new figures that may be emerging from the background of this experience. They use clay and model their own symbol of "This is me right now—the me I am creating and being." I find this a good way to end a particular time-limited gestalt art experience, and I also know that each ending is not an end at all.

My last suggestion to group leaders is to remember that you are a participant, too. You see the group members as individuals. They see you, too. Figure 39 shows some portraits of a male co-leader drawn by four members of a group.

Chapter Ten

WORKING TOGETHER

MAKING A WORLD

Aside from a very few hermits, all of us live in a world in which we continually affect and are affected by the actions of others. We take this for granted, and though we may feel at times like demanding, "Stop the world! I want to get off!" very few of us, of our own accord, get completely off the world. Some of us retreat into our private spaces, refusing or being unable to cope with our environments, either subjectively or objectively. Some of us move from one environment to another, hoping to find one in which we feel at home. Sometimes we succeed in our movings and discover the milieu that suits us best.

But in any living situation, we take with us who we are, and we each contribute to the world the essence and action of us being and doing in relation to others. We make our worlds together. We forget that sometimes and give the other guy both credit and blame that is not his.

In an art experience that is deceptively simply structured, you and others can explore how you affect each other when you work with art materials in one common space that belongs to you all.

I use a large circle cut from heavy wrapping paper as this common space; for eight people, I suggest a circle at least four feet in diameter. I find the best technique is to use collage, which is just pasting down pieces of paper, pictures from magazines, and odds and ends of anything you have around and want to use. Rubber cement in the small jars and cans with brushes attached to their lids is a simple

175

gluing medium. Any white glue works well for attaching pieces of wood, stone, or other heavier materials.

When I offer this activity, I give as few directions as possible. Any group will create an interaction from which directives will evolve naturally from the interchanges among the personalities involved. I can never predict what course this projective experience will take. Sometimes the quietest person in a social situation becomes a rampaging dictator in a world-making exercise; sometimes nobody takes the lead and people cooperate; sometimes people soberly divide the world-space into individual segments and each fills his own part, being very careful not to paste anything on somebody else's imagery; sometimes people paste and throw things all over the circle and utter chaos results instead of cosmos; this triggers anxiety in some people and delight in others. Sometimes people get so interested in each other as people that they forget the paper world and concentrate on the reality of each other.

This art experience is especially valuable for any group whose members are together in living and working situations but who feel stymied in some area of communication. This game is leveling in that disparate roles can be equalized. In families, a 6-year-old can paste his image right on top of Papa's, or maybe Papa will have the sense to support his son's imagery before he gets pasted.

If you care to, try making a world with your family, your colleagues, and/or your friends. You might even try it with your enemies, but I advise that you agree on some basic ground rules before you get into the melee of stuff and glue! No matter how the graphic world turns out, you will learn a great deal about how you all can or can not work together.

TEN WORLDS

I have led all sorts of groups that use art materials, and I might be blasé by now if it weren't that each one is unique. One was sponsored by a suburban community education program. Who would come, from where, and what would they expect? Me, I was expecting chaos; I usually limit my groups to 20 participants, and I prefer only 10. When I learned that 80 people were expected, I yelled "Help!" to my co-leaders, Celia and Norman, and they responded in kind. They are seasoned art group leaders, too, but even so——80 people doing artwork in the same room at the same time?

When we arrived, we spread out ten 4-foot-wide paper circles so they were equally spaced around the school gymnasium where the group was meeting. We asked each of the 80 people to take a plateful of clay from the garbage cans and to seat themselves, eight people to each circle of white paper.

I asked them all to please kindly shut up so I could talk. They did and I did.

"Close your eyes and hold your clay in your hands. Imagine that this clay is the raw material from which you can form whatever you want to put into making a world. You are one of eight people who are going to be making one world. The paper around which you all sit is the empty space on which you will create a fantasy world with the clay forms you make. Let your hands form your individual lump of clay into what you want it to represent, then open your eyes and place your representation on the circle with all the other forms. When all eight of you have put your clay on the circle, open your eyes and begin to work together to structure a whole of the eight parts you have put there. Make any kind of world that seems right for your team of eight co-creators. If you don't agree on what kind of world you want, confront each other with your disagreements, using gestures, words, and acts. Don't harm each other. If you're feeling violent, take it out on the clay, not on a person. If you're feeling loving, caress the clay or another person, depending on how the other feels. Use your good sense, your awareness, and your honesty, and see what sort of world you produce."

While I am speaking, the people are quiet. They really listen. When I stop talking, they begin manipulating the clay, some slowly and uncertainly, others with deft movements that create lifelike models. I look around; everyone seems to be involved. If anyone is thinking, "What a silly thing to be doing on a Friday night!" they don't say so aloud. As they begin putting their individual figures together into one group, the tempo of movement increases, and the noise level rises. Celia, Norman, and I wander around, looking casual but feeling alert for any signs that one of us can facilitate any group's interaction, maybe by encouraging the shy ones to speak out or anticipating worlds about to explode in anger. We do not change any of the action; we go along with any sort of interrelating that seems viable. We confer at times to share our reactions, and then we each join separate groups for as long as we feel our presence contributes something.

Celia joins a group of eight women who sit soberly viewing the flat terrain of their world. "We are tired," they tell her. "We wish we could make a more exciting world, but we don't have the energy. That's sad, but at least we are being honest with each other." The women are listening to themselves and each other; they talk quietly and sometimes chuckle sympathetically.

Celia wisely does not try to interrupt or change their mood; these women have found a common theme in their clay worlds that relates directly with their real-life worlds. They are choosing to share their feelings openly and are doing so in a mutually supportive manner. Celia sits quietly, not saying much, just accepting what is going on as an expression of a natural need for sympathy that we all experience at times. After a while, the women sigh less and laugh more. Celia's contribution to this world is her quiet acceptance; the women are filling their own immediate needs.

I squat by a group whose members seem to be talking all at once. One middle-aged man is holding a clay figure in his hands and protesting vehemently, "But if I can't put my ideals into the world, I won't put in anything at all." He plops his pointed spire right in the center of the world and announces, "That's where idealism belongs! Right in the middle of everything." A long-haired youth retorts, "Oh, man! The world's not ideal; we've got race problems, war, pollution; it won't do any good to stick your static idealism up there. We've got to take drastic action in this world."

I see that there is conflict in this group, but not violence; the only contribution I need to make is to suggest they take time to listen to each other instead of hurrying to speak out for themselves. They are a high-energy group, each one with a lot to say, but they realize that the only way that anyone can be heard is for them to take turns listening. They do this and begin to communicate with more clarity but no less gusto. I leave them. They're doing fine.

Norman is laughing uproariously with another group. A man says, "Look, lady, our world's going to have sex in it whether you like it or not! I won't let you cover up my sex symbol with your silly looking flowers! Take them off me and put them somewhere else!" The lady titters and removes her bouquet from atop the penis she'd mistaken for a stem.

This group is having fun; their laughter is contagious and I join them. Both Norman and I agree that group processes do not have to be somber for the members to gain valuable insights. So we do not dampen spirits by introducing solemn analyses of sexual attitudes. These people are recognizing their different perceptions of what is most important in their individual worlds; they are doing so with honest good humor. They will go home with more assurance that there is space in the world for many different attitudes. Sometimes all we need for relaxed coexistence is to learn to recognize each other's statements as they are intended and find ways to adapt our common space to make room for our inevitable differences.

Interplanetary travel begins. People from one world interpret theirs to the visitors from outer space. In-group cohesion is evident. All kinds of interchanges are going on. Celia, Norman, and I lean against the wall contemplating the scene. As facilitators we are out of business; they don't need us. The participants are experiencing directly in their own way. They don't need any guides to tell them how.

Eleven o'clock. The session is supposed to be over. The janitor comes in scowling. He looks around in disbelief. He leans on his broom, sees those 10 configurations of sculptured clay and hears

80 normal-looking people talking excitedly about worlds. He shakes his head and smiles tolerantly. I imagine that he is thinking: "Well, if people want to spend their time making fancy mud pies and then talking about them as if they're important, that's their business. But I've got a night's work ahead of me." So he turns off all the lights for a few seconds to get attention and then as he flips the switch back on, announces sensibly, "All right, folks. Time to clear out. I've got to clean up this place."

When Celia, Norman, and I reach my home long past midnight, we wonder aloud with each other, "What happened in that session tonight?" Eighty middle-class people, aged 16 to 60, most of them strangers previously, had participated enthusiastically in a game that became reality. They had fun; they learned that they could use art materials; they made contact with others, and they communicated from different points of view with openness and honesty.

We agree: finding joy in immediate experience using art media, making contact and communicating directly with others—that is good! That's what we offer in our brochures, just as many other programs do. All over the country, growth centers, religious groups, business organizations, and schools are supporting group dynamics and are using the same words to describe the positive value of such experiences. We are part of a movement gaining in momentum, and we like what we are doing. But we question also.

For instance, tonight—from that melee of people, clay, paper, talk, and animation—did some participants discover deeper, wider dimensions in themselves and others? Some had said, "I never knew I could speak so freely with others and have them listen to me"; "I certainly learned something about how I act when I work with others"; or simply, "I found out a lot about me!" Will these individual findings affect their daily person-to-person lives when they go back to their too-separate existences?

We wonder and we hope.

A WORLD THAT BLEW APART

Living isn't as easy as it looks; making a world takes some doing. Intelligent, aware, good people find themselves enmeshed in ambiguous, overlapping, interpenetrating, chaotic values and behavior patterns. In creating a paper world, no less than in the actual world, coexistence inevitably elicits unexpected clashes and coalitions.

A consulting psychologist and I co-led the group described next. The 10 members of the group created a world that didn't work. Then we all spent hours upon hours clarifying the implications of what had happened, assimilating what we had learned, and reconciling many apparently conflicting views. We all recognized with honest awe the tremendous problems we live with; we also realized the strengths we can bring to interpersonal relationships when we perceive and respect each other's integrity; we reached a level of group awareness more intense, genuine, and inspiring than I had ever before experienced. We spontaneously closed that last session by saying, all together, "to the Power and the Glory, Amen," without specifying to whom we were singing our praises and without denying either our smiles or our tears.

Later, I received letters from the group members in which they described their individual experiences during those hectic two hours when they were structuring the clay and paper world—50 pages of words that I read with my heart beating faster and faster and my eyes spilling tears. In spite of my intention to edit the letters carefully and present a rational statement of this happening, I couldn't. So I asked Francy Balcomb, my friend and colleague, to read the letters and construct the following composite story of the world that blew apart.

The Group

The group consisted of one advertising executive; one administrative-level educator; two social workers, both administrators with active casework; four religious professionals—one nun, two pastors, one graduate student at a theological seminary; one space-agency industrial engineer who was also an administrator; and one psychologist.

The Situation

An eight-hour-a-day, seven-day group was sponsored by the National Training Laboratories for advancing personal growth following a gestalt approach. Each participant's life indicated a desire for and capability for leadership as well as a desire to mold, form, reconstruct, and motivate others toward a better world. They were professional improvers. It wasn't surprising that all expressed a genuine feeling of pleasant excitement at the prospect of building a world—a new world— together. They all felt they *should* be able to construct a workable and improved world.

The Experience

On the fifth day, the group was presented with a clean table-top to be the world. They had clay, magazine pictures, crayons, scissors, and glue to build with. The personal pleasure of doing the project and the quiet assumption that all would go well and cooperatively left eight of the group silently beginning to explore and construct. They all indicated an awareness of holding back a bit to see what the group wanted. Except two of them. The advertising executive pronounced himself king, while the educator began forming methods of indirectly bringing two very important social questions to the awareness of the group. He felt they had to face the questions of (1) sharing goods, services, and space and (2) defense. He felt happily successful when one of the group picked up his cue and presented a diagram for the allotment of space. His own immediate action had been to wall an area off for himself.

From this point on, it is difficult to describe the experience chronologically. All 10 people were reacting simultaneously—partly against the wall and partly toward their own constructive world-building. The experience breaks down into these stages:

I.   The beginnings
II.   Reactions to the King's offer
III.   The awareness of the wall
IV.   The diagram presented
V.   The wall is attacked
VI.   The bombing
VII.   Three women die
VIII.   The women are asked to return
IX.   The repaired world

The following description will express this simultaneity by grouping everyone's thoughts (as expressed later in their letters) into these various stages of action/reaction.

I.   The beginnings. I felt somewhat apprehensive because I felt we should create a truly new world. . . . I tried to get some feeling as to where I wanted to begin. Power, Autonomy. Me. . . . It all began nicely enough. It seemed obvious that a group effort of some quality and magnitude would emerge. . . . I waited for the choices. . . . I took this task to heart—I was eager but baffled from the start . . . . I stood by the table watching the others take their positions of conviction. . . . I felt high, good, eager: such possibilities, such excitement, such fun. . . . My first feelings were pleasant, joyful ones. I looked forward to the experience with eagerness . . . the opportunity to build our world from scratch and exactly to our liking. Each of us began to obtain or create our representation of what was needed. . . . Rather than raise the question verbally, I just began to build a wall for myself in one corner of the world. At first the others didn't notice what I was doing. . . . Let's build our world—and maybe it'll be so beautiful he'll want to join us.

II. Reactions to the King's offer. I remember Ed wise-cracking, "I want to build this world only if I can proclaim myself King right now." Somebody said, not very amused, "No Kings!". . . . One has quickly decided that he would be king, even before we had really begun developing our world. . . . He was ignored by the group. He became frustrated as the others progressed without him—and he stood by. . . . Nobody seemed to take seriously Ed's grandiose offer to head up the project. Still, though, a few of us expressed a need for some sense of direction.

III. The awareness of the wall. Then I saw Jim to my left. His body filled with energy; he was building a wall. I didn't want it there. With playfulness I didn't feel in the growing tightness in my chest and stomach, I reached over and began to poke holes in the wall. He turned on me. His face contorted with fury. . . . I was stunned, refusing to believe it was a defense. . . . My immediate response was retaliation. . . . I had seen it out of the corner of my eye, but now I turned to face it head on. . . . To me it was at once an affront and a challenge. . . . He was now saying to me, "I don't need you." I was mad as hell and a little afraid, for he was a powerfully built man, and his eyes were moist, and other signs clearly indicated that what he was feeling was intense. . . . My fear won out over my anger. . . . I defended myself against my feelings by involving myself again with the rest of the group. . . . I was really disturbed. I felt shocked and troubled. . . . Together we tried to talk him out of it. . . . No one liked the wall and said so. . . . One of the members of the group was putting up a wall, fort-like in appearance, and was beginning to shape round balls that I interpreted to be missiles. I challenged him on this. . . . I became suddenly angry. . . . When they became aware of my wall, several invited me to join the group—to take down my wall and build a stockpile of mutually owned resources with the rest. It was apparent that all of the others were disgusted with my behavior and were going to freeze me out of the group.

IV. The diagram presented. Denis apparently saw what I was leading up to, and he took some crayons and sketched out a model world—his world had a private place for everybody and a general area for common use. . . . Denis produced a diagram of a plan—this was by way of a compromise. He hoped that Jim would make his walled-in place a part of the general plan. . . . Bob or someone began to conciliate. I wasn't hearing anything clearly. . . . I felt frustrated, but it was at a low level because I counted heavily on Denis' design, trusting that in some freewheeling way we would sort out our separate contributions and get our central world together. . . . It seemed a good solution to the problem raised by Jim, and we went on with our building. . . . Jim would have none of this.

V. The wall is attacked. Suddenly Carter had had it. She threw something at Jim angrily. . . . I suddenly became very angry. I reached for a piece of clay, carefully rounded it into a ball, and leveled it squarely at Jim's wall. Yes, I was seething inside, but I was also laughing as I hurled the clay. . . . Again I was stunned. I could feel the time pressure—the immediacy—with almost no time to come to basic agreements. I was uncomfortable with that feeling, which evolved into discouragement and disgust. I was mad again because the disruptiveness was inhibiting. I was beginning to smell defeat. . . . I was stunned.

VI. The bombing. I made not one bomb but many small ones and several large ones. I stole clay from the common supply and made a secret cache of bombs that I stuck on the underside of the table. No one paid any attention to me during this period; they were ignoring me intentionally and freezing me out. . . . Our concentration was shattered by a loud noise from behind the wall, a shout, "These are BOMBS". . . . He picked up his balls of clay and one by one hurled them forcefully at the center of the table and then grabbed with both hands all he could hold of the precious representations of what we wanted built into our world. His eyes were afire. He was almost in a rage. And by now the rest of us were furious, too. His fists were clenched. I was on the verge of panic. . . . I stood by in uncertainty and bewilderment, but definitely determined that each should arm himself. . . . I was dumbfounded. I felt hopeless. . . . As he bombarded, I began guerilla activities. I took my scissors and actually began to cut off his corner. Bob said, "Don't". . . . I felt angry at him and demanded to know what he was doing. When I learned he was making a kind of attack on us and had even gone so far as to make bombs, I could scarcely believe it! My first impulse was hostile and aggressive—to grab him and physically force him to stop what he was doing. . . . I was disbelieving. I looked at his face, and I was afraid. Could I fight back? No, I had no weapons. Bombs were coming faster. What chance was there? No sense fighting back—that'll ruin the world anyway. . . . Something hit the pile. I heard or thought it was a bomb, but it was so unreal, and I continued building the world. He would grab. Then his hand covered everything, snatched it up, squeezed it all into a blob mass, and put it behind his wall. All was gone. Where was I? I was left in limbo. . . . I expected the group to get the message—the looks on their faces were almost frightening to me. I think I really got emotionally involved in the experience for the first time at that point. I saw an expression of mixed unbelief and revulsion on his face. Every fiber of his body was withdrawing from me—and I realized things were going in a direction I did not like at all. . . . That moment was a peak of confusion and fear I had not known before. What had started as a game had turned into a terrifying nightmare, only it was so real!

VII.   Three women die. Then Jim saw my clay figure close to his wall on the table and said, "Oh, no you don't, Lady," and I got hit right off, wiped out. There was no time to explain; it was too late, I was gone, dead, stunned, and shaking like crazy. I was killed. Funny, but it was almost a relief. . . . Madeline said she was dead. I was in limbo and didn't know what to do so I joined her in thinking about dying. I knew I could go back and play in the world-making process, and I thought with some calculation that the others would think me heroic if I were to die. But then I was unsure. Someplace on the edge of my consciousness I knew that to play dead was somehow to face my own death. It became very important to me to stay dead. . . . I found myself in the company of Thelma and Carter. They, too, had been wiped out. We sat very close at first, then we shared. I had done all I could do, and I was dead. Free—yes, I knew I was free. . . . The death experience was strange for me. I was cold, sad—yes, relieved—but most strongly guilty. I had played a major role in precipitating this war, this pain and confusion. . . . I told Carter that I felt some space between us, and she wryly said she was in purgatory. I didn't want to join them in thinking about, worrying, wanting for those in the other world. I wanted to enjoy death. . . . Suddenly three members of the group said that they had been killed and withdrew completely. . . . They said that they were no longer in our world because they were dead—they had been killed! This immediately terrified me because I had been so dependent on the cooperation, the coordination of our group. I felt a tremendous loss and depression because I didn't know how to persuade them that the world must go on and their place was in it. It was as if they didn't hear me.

VIII.   The women are asked to return. Others spoke, and Jim seemed to understand what he had done. Three girls had renounced themselves from the world. Jim wanted them back and wanted others to ask them to return to him. . . . Jim explained and explained. He asked them point blank. They repeated that they were dead and could not return. . . . With tears in her eyes, and with a kind of agonized intensity, Madeline said, "I'm dead. I can't come back. I put myself on the line, and you killed me." They felt dead. They were dead. Our world would have to go on without them. . . . In a little while the men turned back to building, and, as I stood helplessly, agonizingly trying to think of new ways to persuade the three dead ones to come back, one of the men said wistfully, "Come on Bee; we can't do without a woman in the world." As I turned back to the table, I was actually dizzy and faint. I thought I might have to lie down, and I gripped the edge of the table and took deep breaths. I felt mournful. I felt very much aware of the fact that I, the only woman left in the world, was past childbearing age. It seemed very real that mankind was soon to die out.

IX.   The repaired world. Reluctantly and sadly I returned to the table with the others. The enthusiasm was drained out of me, and I felt resigned to make the best of a bad situation. . . . The rest was an anticlimax for me. . . . I remember that one individual cut off a little piece of cardboard and, putting it into his pocket, sat on the floor for the rest of the time. . . . Our world was a little messy, but we were on our way. In time we would clean up. . . . I had some feeling of satisfaction that the men had only an old woman in their world and couldn't procreate. As if somehow I had a victory. . . . Our sloppy, messy, but increasingly interesting world. . . . I felt that I just had to get out of the world that had been created. I picked up the scissors, cut off a small piece of the world, and moved away from the world; I felt very detached, a small segment detached from myself. . . . I rooted for them in my heart; I hoped they'd make it. It seemed rather pathetic that they were asking the same questions we'd asked before the war. I longed for them.

BUILDING A WORLD

Building a world with other people is one way of discovering yourself in process with other people in the world. It can be a moving, upsetting, and even uplifting experience. After building a world, we often find it necessary to withdraw into ourselves in order to assimilate our social actions, outbursts, and repressions in relation to that non-public person we also experience as ourselves.

Just as the world-building experience was too simultaneous for a clear, ordered, and linear account of it, our own processes are too simultaneous for easy understanding of what we are and how much we are. Sometimes all we can assimilate is that we *are* in process.

The world that blew apart was a clay and paper world, but it was created by people of flesh, blood, and bone. Though this fragile, imaginary world was destroyed, its creators were not. They were startled, bewildered, even frightened when they looked at the messy debris littering a makeshift studio and realized how much they had expressed and experienced—how deeply they had affected each other's lives.

We all knew that what had happened was more than a childish game. What we had experienced was real—we can blow our world apart, we just might do it; we can whimper our way into extinction; we can fight each other into numbed attrition. We can do lots of things. We are pretty powerful creatures, and we have available many ways to use our power. Unless we mess up our spaceship earth so that it is not fit to live on, or unless some other power pulls rank on us, we're the ones who have the responsibility of making what we can of this space we share. When our common forebears munched on the apple of knowledge and were kicked out of innocence, they handed us a world-game that takes quite a bit of perceptiveness to understand and play with wisdom and grace.

Until something happens to prove otherwise, I'm saying we can find what we need to play that game to create better worlds—even when we have to use the scraps left over from the world we blew apart.

Appendix: Materials

PAPER

Sheet Paper

When buying paper, keep in mind what drawing media you will use on the paper and that the paper should be inexpensive enough so no one feels inhibited by its cost. Some of the paper should be heavy enough so that when two or more people are drawing at the same time, it won't tear easily. Manila or white construction paper works well for this purpose. Newsprint is fine for quick oil pastel drawings but is too thin for poster paint work.

Make available various sizes of paper:

Typing paper, 8½" × 11". Can be purchased from any variety or stationery store. The cheaper the better—cheaper paper has a rougher surface and thus takes crayons and chalks better. Buy lots.

Manila paper, 24" × 36". Buff-colored, heavy, toothed paper in medium weight. Priced to meet low budgets, it is an excellent paper for pencil, chalk, pastels, crayons, brush, and ink sketches.

Extra-rough manila paper, 24" × 36". A very coarse finish—sometimes known as oatmeal paper. Good for chalks, pastels, crayons, and pencil. The best I know has the trade name "Alphatone," which comes in sheets and rolls. Best source is school supply stores.

Newsprint, 18" × 24" or 24" × 36". Especially suited for dry media, yet gives interesting results with inks and water colors.

White construction paper, 18" × 24" or 24" × 36". Fairly heavy, white paper that will hold up under poster paint or can be used for paper sculpture.

White school drawing paper. All-purpose white paper. Very similar to white construction paper.

Paper for finger painting. You can buy this in an art or school supply store, but it is fairly expensive. Adequate substitutes are any slick nonabsorbent paper. Plastic-coated shelf lining paper is excellent. For group work in finger painting I use a 4' × 8' sheet of paneling that is coated with a white plastic surface into which the colors will not penetrate. The dried paints can be hosed off later and the board re-used. Some of the people may have to be hosed off, too. Finger painting together can be a very messy activity but sometimes it is thoroughly satisfying in encouraging playful interaction.

Paper Rolls

Newsprint rolls. Roll ends can be purchased very cheaply from newspaper printing plants. They come in various widths depending on the size of the plants' presses.

Butcher paper rolls. White, very similar to white shelf paper, but a little heavier. This paper is heavier than newsprint and has a much slicker surface. It is very good for poster paints and not so good for chalks. Butcher paper comes in various widths—18, 24, 36, and 48 inches. It usually has to be purchased through a paper house or by an art store through a school supply house. If you have a friendly butcher, you can sometimes buy rolls from him, but these will generally be only the 18" width.

Wrapping paper rolls. Brown, about the same weight as butcher paper. Small rolls can be purchased from a variety store. Larger (wider and longer) rolls can be ordered through paper houses or art stores.

Shelf paper. Comes in various colors, textures, and finishes, with adhesive and plain backing. It is excellent for finger painting and for other water paints since its non-porous surface keeps the colors from soaking into the paper. Slick shelf papers are no good for crayons, chalks, or cray-pas, however.

Paper for Collages

Heavyweight paper for the base: cut-up cardboard boxes or chipboard are great. White construction paper will do also. In gathering materials for collage try for the greatest variety possible. The only limiting factor should be whether it can be glued down.

Multi-colored construction paper. Can be purchased in most variety stores in packets.

Tissue paper. Cheap wrapping tissue comes in various colors; no need to buy the super art-store tissue papers unless you covet their color selection (which is gorgeous).

Old wallpaper sample books. Can be acquired by beseeching paint and wallpaper stores.

Magazines. Choose those that offer the richest variety of color and black and white photos.

Comic books. Get a variety. From *Little Lulu* to *Marvel's Thor* and various Superman-type comics. The more absurd the better.

Cloth scraps. Start collecting, looking for a variety of texture, pattern, and color. Also pick up scrap yarns and colored strings (sometimes people do feel strung out).

CHALKS, CRAYONS

Cray-pas, or oil pastels, give a rich color. Their oil base makes it possible to blend them easily and makes them soft enough to give a good hard, deep color as well as a soft, tentative color.

Crayons. Regular school crayons are not too good—they are a bit chintzy with their color and tend to demand to be used mainly on the tips. Oil pastels can be used broadly or pointedly with equal ease. Japanese oil pastels are the best for the money. You can buy them in discount, drug, and variety stores as well as art stores. Be sure to strip off the paper covers so you can use the whole tool.

Chalks. The best are the large fist-sized colored chalks. They offer a good variety of color, and people can get a real hold on them. Freart chalks are the largest ones I have been able to find. The cover of this book shows Freart chalks used on a tennis court. I believe the only way to get Freart chalks is through a school supply store or by writing to the manufacturer, The American Crayon Company, Sandusky, Ohio.

A good fixative for chalks is the cheapest hair spray you can find (the cheapest ones have the most lacquer). Spray the drawing two or three times from about 15 inches away.

FLOW PENS

Again, there are many kinds of felt-tip pens. A water-based ink is the best for your purposes and is often the least expensive. Get lots, and get a good color selection. If the pens dry out, you can reactivate them by dipping the tips in a dish of water for a few moments. The white flow pens are not particularly good. The ink dries too quickly.

POSTER PAINTS

Buy dry pigments and mix your own. The best way to mix them is to pour the pigment in a jar, add water slowly until the whole thing is mixed to a thick glop, then add water to desired consistency. Most people prefer thicker paints, which they can thin if desired as they work.

Any brand is okay. Usually, the cheaper the pigments, the more extender used. This means that you may be sacrificing some color intensity in buying the cheaper ones, but the difference is certainly not important at first.

SUMI INK IN LIQUID FORM

If you are lucky enough to know of an oriental shop—art, stationery, or even a variety store—you can buy sumi ink in pint and quart sizes. Mixed with water, either in small containers or on the paper itself, the ink will flow from deep black to marvelously delicate grays. It can be used on almost any paper with different effects, of course. When applied to a damp sheet of paper, the flowing shapes that emerge naturally are so fascinating that novices forget their fearfulness of letting lines and shapes happen.

GLUES

White glue. Elmer's, Borden's, and other brands are a plastic glue made from milk products. They dry clear and hold very well if the objects have good contact while they are drying. White glue thinned with water is the easiest way to put down tissue paper. Brush it approximately where you expect to put the tissue, place the tissue, and then brush over the top. The glue saturates from both sides of the paper this way and holds very well.

Rubber cement. Good for paper and for materials that don't keep good contact while drying. If you paint both objects, let them dry, and then put them together, you will get a very strong bond. Using the cement wet will also hold well. Buy enough small dispensers with brushes so at least every two to three people can share. You can refill these from quart cans. The rubber cement solvent is used for thinning and is necessary to keep on hand as rubber cement quickly gets too rubbery.

BRUSHES

Japanese bamboo brushes and cheap natural bristle house painter's brushes (about 1½″ × 2″) will give you the two extremes in size. Fill in the middle with stiff-bristle oil painting brushes and some soft-haired rounds. It is important to give yourself a good size selection in brushes.

CERAMIC CLAY

This clay comes in premixed plugs of 25 to 50 pounds. (Use about 10 pounds per person for group sessions; at least 25 pounds should be kept on hand when one is working at home.) I advise getting the red earth clays—the white clay looks and feels very artificial and man-made. Get in touch with the earth. Add water to the clay when it starts to dry and work it some to soften it up. I usually store my clay in a large plastic bucket with a tight lid. I cover the clay with wet rags and wet burlap if I know that I won't be using it for a few weeks.

It is useful to have a board approximately 18″ × 18″ as a base for the clay work. Any smooth-surfaced material like masonite or plastic will do.

SCISSORS

A supply of small, inexpensive scissors, preferably sufficiently pointed so that tiny details can be cut exactly by those who feel a need for neatness.

SHEARS

At least one pair of shears for quickly cutting lengths from the larger rolls of paper.

ROLLS OF WIRE

Copper, aluminum, picture wire, any kind that people can use for tying things together or for hanging mobiles. Your local hardware store probably has various kinds of wire.

VARIOUS CONTAINERS

Paper cups, large cans for washing brushes, and small jars with lids for keeping liquid poster paints. Cultivate friends with infants —baby-food jars make perfect containers for paints.

Of course you may not want, need, or have space for all of these materials. They *do* make quite a clutter!

In my studio—in which we are continually organizing the chaotic clutter—I also have baskets and boxes of non-categorizable materials such as sticks, stones, beads, rusty nails, bits of intriguingly shaped metal, straw mats, twigs, ribbons, seeds, beans, dried leaves, miniature plastic figures of animals, people, machines, and so on.

Accumulate these at your own risk. They may fill up your studio space so that people can't find the other materials they want. However, I find when I offer access to such a large variety of materials, persons often discover a material with which they intuitively identify: they recognize some part of what they need to express but hadn't realized until they saw the object.

So I choose to keep the clutter around and available to participants on open shelves as much as possible.

I make these suggestions about materials knowing that your situation and desires and common sense will determine what materials are best for you.

Bibliography

American Journal of Art Therapy, 1961–1973.

Arnheim, R., *Art and Visual Perception.* Berkeley: University of California Press, 1966.

Arnheim, R., *Visual Thinking.* Berkeley: University of California Press, 1969.

Arnheim, R., *Toward a Psychology of Art.* Berkeley: University of California Press, 1972.

Barron, F., *Creativity and Personal Freedom,* rev. ed. New York: Van Nostrand Reinhold, 1968.

Barron, F., *Creative Person and Creative Process.* New York: Holt, Rinehart & Winston, 1969.

Barron, F., and Child, I. L., "The Creative Explosion," *Psychology Today,* December, 1968.

Boas, F., *Primitive Art.* New York: Dover, 1955.

Bugental, J. F. T., ed., *Challenges of Humanistic Psychology.* New York: McGraw-Hill, 1967.

Camus, A., *The Rebel.* New York: Alfred A. Knopf, 1954.

Carpenter, E., *They Became What They Beheld.* New York: Ballantine, 1970.

Egan, G., *Encounter.* Monterey, Calif.: Brooks/Cole, 1970.

Fagan, J., and Shepherd, I. L., eds., *Gestalt Therapy Now.* Palo Alto, Calif.: Science and Behavior Books, 1970.

Fallico, A. B., *Art and Existentialism.* Englewood Cliffs, N.J.: Prentice-Hall, 1962.

Fuller, B., *Ideas and Integrities.* Englewood Cliffs, N.J.: Prentice-Hall, 1963.

Ghiselin, B., ed., *The Creative Process.* Berkeley: University of California Press, 1952.

Hall, E., *The Silent Language.* New York: Doubleday, 1959.

Horney, K., *Neurosis and Human Growth.* New York: W. W. Norton, 1950.

Itten, J., *Design and Form—The Basic Course at the Bauhaus.* New York: Van Nostrand Reinhold, 1964.

Journal of Humanistic Psychology, 1960–1973.

Jung, C. G., *The Undiscovered Self.* Boston: Little, Brown, 1957.

Jung, C. G., *Psyche and Symbol.* New York: Doubleday, 1958.

Jung, C. G., *Man and His Symbols.* New York: Doubleday, 1964.

Kellogg, R., and O'Dell, S., *The Psychology of Children's Art.* New York: Random House, 1967.

Koffka, K., *Principles of Gestalt Psychology.* New York: Harcourt Brace Jovanovich, 1935.

Kohler, W., *Dynamics in Psychology.* New York: Liveright, 1940.

Kohler, W., *Gestalt Psychology.* New York: Liveright, 1947.

Kris, E., *Psychoanalytic Explorations in Art.* New York: International University Press, 1952.

Kubie, L. S., *Neurotic Distortion of the Creative Process.* Kansas City: University of Kansas Press, 1958.

Langer, S. K., *Philosophy in a New Key.* Cambridge: Harvard University Press, 1942.

Lehner, E., *The Picture Book of Symbols.* New York: William Penn Publishing, 1956.

May, R., "Our Schizoid World," *Psychology Today,* August, 1969.

McKim, R., *Experiences in Visual Thinking.* Monterey, Calif.: Brooks/Cole, 1972.

McLuhan, M., *Understanding Media: The Extensions of Man.* New York: McGraw-Hill, 1964.

Naumburg, M., *Dynamically Oriented Art Therapy.* New York: Grune & Stratton, 1966.

Perls, F. S., *Ego, Hunger and Aggression.* New York: Random House, 1969.

Perls, F. S., *Gestalt Therapy Verbatim.* Moab, Ut.: Real People Press, 1969.

Perls, F. S., Hefferline, R. F., and Goodman, P., *Gestalt Therapy.* New York: Julian Press, 1951.

Peterson, S., *A Catalog of the Ways People Grow.* New York: Ballantine Books, 1971.

Pursglove, P. D., ed., *Recognitions in Gestalt Therapy.* New York: Harper & Row, 1971.

Read, H., *A Concise History of Modern Painting.* New York: Praeger, 1959.

Read, H., *The Forms of Things Unknown.* New York: World, 1963.

Rilke, R. M., *Letters to a Young Poet.* New York: W. W. Norton, 1934.

Robertson, S. M., *Rosegarden and Labyrinth.* London: Routledge & Kegan Paul, 1963.

Rogers, C. R., *On Becoming a Person.* Boston: Houghton Mifflin, 1970.

Singer, J., and Hall, M. H., "Focus on Fantasy," *Psychology Today,* April, 1968.

Sutich, A., and Vich, M. A., *Readings in Humanistic Psychology.* New York: The Free Press, 1969.

Weintraub, D. J., and Walker, E. L., *Perception.* Monterey, Calif.: Brooks/Cole, 1966.

Weltfish, G., *The Origins of Art.* New York: Bobbs-Merril, 1953.

Whitmont, E. C., *The Symbolic Quest.* New York: G. P. Putnam's Sons, 1969.

Whyte, L. L., *The Next Development in Man.* New York: The New American Library, 1950.

Whyte, L. L., ed., *Aspects of Form.* London: Percy Lund Humphries, 1951.

Index